RE-THINKING VALUES IN AFRICA: FOR COLLECTIVE WELL-BEING

BAWA KUYINI

DEDICATION

This Book is dedicated to my parents
Mahama Abu Kuyini and Samata Kuyini

TABLE OF CONTENTS

i

Chapter 1
Introduction

"Anything that is added to your being, which is not a slap on the
face, is not something to worry about"

(A proverb from the Dagomba people of Ghana)

Africa, a continent that conjures images of disease, hunger, war and
savagery in the minds of outsiders is also a continent full of simple
humanity. It still holds large pockets of the traditional humane
values that much of the world has lost. There is an ocean of
generosity that moves Africans to welcome and care for strangers/
visitors without pretence and this act of generosity is genuine,
demonstrating complete acceptance of our common humanity.
However, the reality of the daily struggle to survive is often not too
far away. It comes knocking every single hour when people wonder
where they are going to find the next meal; when children die before
their prime from simple illnesses and when you have to attend
funerals nearly every day. These are glaring reminders of life's
vulnerabilities in Africa; something you forget when you live in
London or New York. They are the profound realities of Africa's
unfulfilled promise - at independence - to create better conditions for
her peoples.

In 2001, British Prime Minister Tony Blair referred to the African
condition as "a scar on the conscience of the world". His statement
offended many Africans and a prominent Ghanaian politician
commented that we (Africans) do not need Britain to save us; after
all it was the same Britain who robbed and exploited us for hundreds
of years. These "proud Africans" who claim that Africa is capable of
minding its own affairs are, however, totally silent on the ills caused
by greedy and corrupt politicians who have held the populations to
ransom, delivering nothing to improve general wellbeing for over 50
years.

The fundamental reason for writing a book about the conditions of
the African people, which many more eloquent non-African writers
have already written about, is a belief that subjective African
opinions of this state of affairs can provide a new way of looking at
the issues. Therefore central to my writing this book is a desire to
present an insider (an African) rather than outsider

1

(European/American) view of the African condition, which rests on a social constructivist perspective of reality. In this process, I hold the strong view that Africa cannot justifiably continue to blame the West for its current failures. This position is underpinned by the fact that the impact of colonialism in Africa was not different from the experiences of colonialism in some parts of Asia and yet African societies today can be characterised as nothing more than "kingdoms of hell with a million prayers". And the journey onto these kingdoms of hell began with unimaginable high hopes of a better future.

Further, my desire has been precipitated by the fact that reality is socially constructed and this is in line with Paulo Friere's ideas around emancipation. In my view, it is important to construct an internal African reality. As an African, my construction of the African condition shares similarity with others who have experienced it and thought about how things could have been different. As a child growing under those terrible conditions and now living in a western industrialised nation, I have faced many questions from friends and colleagues about Africa's problems. There is often an expression of both contempt and pity for Africa and such reactions to my continent of birth are quite unpleasant; sometimes, depressing. I believe that self-pity should be the point of departure between resignation and real action and to me that kind of action is sharing my thoughts, however irrelevant they may seem to others. My experiences, observations, thoughts and frustrations have been gradually synthesised into a set of ideas, which is presented in this book. I am aware that criticizing my own society can be perceived by some people are being arrogant as Leopold Senghor experienced in his interpretation of African philosophy. Professor Valentin.Y. Mudimbe writes in his book *The invention of Africa* that Senghor had been accused (by African intellectuals such as Wole Soyinka) of seeking to promote a detestable model for a division of vocations between Africa and Europe, between African and European, simply because Senghor had suggested to members of his Senegalese Socialist Party in July 1963 that many Africans lacked an awareness of their own poverty and creative imagination - the spirit of resourcefulness.

In order to avoid this perception I present my ideas in a "We" and "Our" format, demonstrating that I am part of the problem, and also part of the solution. I do not see this book as the solution and so I am ready to accept that perhaps this work might not make any contribution at all to Africa's attempt to overcome our collective tribulations, because some people will dismiss my ideas. But that in itself is something that will speak to the nature of the African condition, the propensity to dismiss ideas not coming from outside. Most of us know quite well that life in many communities in Africa, is akin to living in a hell where millions of prayers are heard unceasingly asking for relief from God, the supernatural. However, the pragmatic alternatives before us are left unexplored simply because we fail to interrogate the everyday inactions and failures of each and every one of us. This book is an attempt to do exactly that, by bringing to the fore everyday things that have profound and lasting negative effects on Africa's capacity to create the kingdoms of heaven promised by independence and de-colonization.

The abolition of slavery had set the stage for "re-humanising" the African; discounting the notion that Africans were an inferior race. Indeed when the American colonization society began the move to resettle freed slaves in the 19th Century in Africa, they harped on a more positive image of the Negro, which departed from the popular /prevailing subhuman or inferior human thesis/argument. However, this "re-humanisation" was only at the political level among the perpetrators of slavery. It was another 100 years before the next step in Africa's "re-humanisation" took place when nearly all of the colonies of Africa gained independence in the early 1960s. Decolonisation was a true watershed in Africa's "re-humanisation" and self-determination. Frantz Fanon encapsulated this in his Wretched of the Earth" when he wrote:

"Decolonization never takes place unnoticed, for it influences individuals and modifies them fundamentally. It transforms spectators crushed with their inessentiality into privileged actors, with the grandiose glare of history's floodlights upon them. It brings a natural rhythm into existence, introduced by new men, and with it a new language and a new humanity. Decolonization is the veritable creation of new men. But this creation owes nothing of its legitimacy to any supernatural power; the "thing" which has been colonized becomes man during the same process by which it frees itself "(p. 36).

Indeed, independence provided the platform for self-determination and a chance to prove that "the Blackman is capable of managing his own affairs" (Kwame Nkrumah, first president of Ghana's famous statement in his independence speech, 6 March 1957). As the first independent country in sub-Saharan Africa, Ghana, propelled by the ideology self-determination and new national identity, pursued policies that gave birth to liberation successes across Africa. At the beginning of the 1960s several other African nations including

3

Guinea, Kenya, Uganda, Tanzania, Nigeria, and Mali, following in the footsteps of Ghana gained independence from colonial rule and sought to project messages of freedom, self-pride and self-determination. In the Caribbean and the Americas the bright fires of the African independence reinforced the drive to secure civil rights and prominent figures such as Martin Luther King Jr. and Malcolm X echoed the messages of black freedom and nationalism delivered earlier by Marcus Garvey, W.E.B Du Bois, George Padmore and others. By the late 1960s, Reggae Musicians like Jimmy Cliff and Bob Marley preached the message of equality and the Black nations' potential to deliver better living conditions for their peoples.

However, the direction and strength of the "freedom current" was not very clear because there were pockets of doubts about the "Africa can go it alone" discourse that dominated the thinking of African leaders and some elite. This could be discerned from actions and dealings of many African leaders with their colonial masters and tribalism killing nationalism in the young nations. At the core of the African leaders' political and educational agenda was an expressed identification with the post-colonial notion of Ambivalence, which writers like Leela Gandhi refer to as a complex mix of attraction and repulsion that characterises the colonial and post-colonial relationship. Such a position was and is fostered because according to Stuart Hall (writing about the dominance of western power), "Western colonial power possesses powerful symbolic appeal for non-western others, constituting the seemingly universal standard of human aesthetics, cultural values and social progress to which non-western others are compelled to conform 'not only as a matter of imposed will and domination, but by the power of inner compulsion and subjective conformation to the norm' (Hall, 1990, in Hooks, 1992, p.3). However, Leela Ghandi, Keita Takayama and Michael Apple writing about the appeal of colonial power argued that in spite of this strong appeal, non-western nations have both an attraction to and repulsion towards the west and such reactions /responses to western ideas and discourses are common among nationalists in non-western nations.

In a parallel attitude and action akin to what Richard Fox (1992) calls *Affirmative Orientalism*, African leaders, notably Kwame Nkrumah (Ghana), Julius Nyerere (Tanzania) and Sekou Toure (Guinea) tried to redefine Africa's position in relation to the west. For Nkrumah, his famous saying 'the Blackman is capable of managing his own Affairs' (Independence Speech, 6 March 1957) was a definitive statement, followed by the Africanisation of national institutions and the educational curriculum. Riding on the euphoric wave of freedom and self-determination, Nkrumah, tried to conceptualise education as a vehicle for crystallizing new national goals and visions. The attraction and repulsion of the West was apparent in situating the educational discourse within the framework of western cultural imperialism. And this understanding witnessed the Nkrumah Government's attempt to indigenise the curriculum through the use of Ghanaian languages and new reading materials. Graduates of Ghana's educational system were to become, in Nkrumah's vision, a pioneering example of an educated and skilled population running an emerging, healthy African industrial economy - an answer to Europe and America, and a foundation for a true African emancipation. The anti-colonialists ideology, embedded in the notion of ambivalence also crystallised into the slogan of self-reliance, and was pragmatised in the policies of import substitution and the 'Operation Feed Yourself Program' which Ghana pursued into the 1970s.

In Tanzania, Julius Nyerere developed his famous Ujamaa Project, which also saw the adoption of Swahili as a national language and the main medium of instruction in schools. In Guinea, Sekou Toure was determined to erase French influence on the Guinean society. This led to his country's suspension from the Franco-phone West African group of nations.

However, nearly 60 years after the euphoria of independence and self-determination, the carving out of economic and material development to uplift the general wellbeing of the population has not been realised. Africa is dependent on aid from former colonial masters and although many development experts believe that aid, investment and education will lead to the economic emancipation of Africa, the magnitude of inequality and marginalisation of the vast majority of the population requires a re-cast of the potential remedy to Africa's problems and the re-orientation of the prevailing values across the African continent.

Professor Ali Mazrui's work, which urges retraditionalization of Africa, might be the way forward. And V. Y. Mudimbe rightly observes that retraditionalization is not Westernisation but Mordernisation because retraditionalization of African culture can take modernizing forms, especially if it becomes an aspect of decolonization. Retraditionalization does not mean returning Africa to what it was before Europeans came...But a move towards renewed respect for indigenous ways and the conquest of cultural self-contempt may be the minimal conditions for cultural decolonization (Mudimbe, 169). "Retraditionalization" Ali Mazrui holds, would be one more version of Africa re-inventing itself.

Overview of content

In this book I intend to discuss briefly Africa's glory and her current tribulations, including a crisis of values, before I sketch alternative ideas about values that will enable Africa's progress. First, I discuss the common and sometimes superficial factors that are proclaimed to explain the African condition. These include the generally predictable natural environment of the African continent and the lack of broad and extensively shared collective experiences and values, which are usually brought forth by vast and enduring empires that bind together large populations. I then highlight the tragic failure of independent governments to reconstruct the paths to a glorious destiny for the populations and note extreme examples such as Nigeria, Zaire and Rwanda. I then try to espouse a number of factors, including values, which lie beyond economics and which have been marginalised in the discourse of the African malaise. These include values of community and the notion of Affirmative Subjugation. I also focus attention on our extreme adherence to prayer and miracles in religious practice to the exclusion of other essential values such as honesty and responsibility, which implies that we have little understanding of the conscience of religion. And I argue that:

Africans' practice of religion, indeed our faith and prayers, qualify to be defined (in the words of Ambrose Bierce) as a request to God that the laws of the universe be annulled on behalf of petitioners (Africans) who are confessedly unworthy of God's Mercy".

In exploring these underlying issues, I make the argument that Africa is experiencing many tribulations, which follows hundreds of years of glory and 400 years of suffering, abuse and exploitation. However, it is not impossible to overcome these tribulations if positive values are cultivated and I argue for re-valuing Africa in the domains of thought and approach to life, beliefs and religious practice, politics and education. If we do not do this and allow destructive religious practices and unreasonable allegiance to tribes to anesthetise our capacity to stand up to our corrupt leaders, we cannot blame the West for our collective failure. Such an outcome will certainly solidify the case that the African condition is a self-

6

imposed destiny. And destiny, Ambrose Bierce noted, is 'A tyrant's authority for crime and a fool's excuse for failure'.

Caveat: why Africa cannot be analysed as a single entity

Africa is so diverse and any attempt at a monolithic and unifying discourse about the continent is certainly too simplistic. Even a book such as this one, which concentrates on Sub-Saharan Africa, will be unable to justify any broad generalisations because West, Southern and East Africa have very different characteristics in terms of culture, including language, food, arts and music. However, two factors that unite these different sections of Africa are their common colonial experience and collective failure (of the more than 50 countries) to move beyond poverty and provide better living conditions for their peoples. In this regard any generalised descriptions of Africa and its people in the subsequent pages, are more or less broad strokes, which in no way necessarily imply that Africa is devoid of exceptions.

PART I: AFRICA IN AND OUT OF GLORY

Chapter 2:
Challenging popular narratives of Africa's history

Brief history

Long before the coming of the trans-Saharan slave trade, Africa was almost an unknown land. Much of what was known of Africa was limited to North Africa - Egypt, Sudan, and Ethiopia. Black people played a key role in the pyramid civilization as evidenced in the Nubian areas of southern Egypt and Sudan. Another well-documented aspect of this is the influence of Abyssinia from the pre-Christian era to the period of the Islamic renaissance in East Africa. It is common knowledge that African Queens of power ruled kingdoms, which played key roles at different times in history. These great rulers include the Queens of Ethiopia; Queen of Sheba (960 B.C.), Candace of Meroe who defeated Alexander the Great (332 B.C.), Amanirenas (40-10 BC) and Nubian Queens Amanishakhete (10-0 B.C.) and Amanitore (1-20 AD). In particular the story of King Solomon of Israel and the Queen of Sheba, which embodies the history of the Ethiopian Jews, is undoubtedly nearly as old as Judaic history. Then in about 615 AD the Prophet of Islam Mohammed sought refuge with the Christian King (Negus) of Abyssinia and this became the turning point in the survival story of the Islamic religion. The nature of King Negus' kingdom, his values of hospitality and the significance of his support have never been lost to or forgotten by Muslim scholars. It has been engraved in history and lauded as Africa's unique and indispensable contribution to the existence of Islam today.

There are some scholars who discount the role of black Africans in this epoch of human history. These critics maintain that light-skinned people built the pyramids and by this, they ignore the fact that the many pyramids within the Nubian empires were built entirely by black kings. There is evidence that Nubian kings built great pyramids along the Nile valley and only during the construction of the Aswan dam were many of these great and unique monuments destroyed or lost to humanity. The African populations along the Nile were astute in agricultural technology, including the domestication of animals and the use of iron.

To counter this denial of African antiquity, many theories have been proposed principal among them, the Afrocentrists' Theory of Stolen Legacy. This theory advances the argument that the Greeks plagiarized African philosophy and made it their own. Due to the controversies surrounding this theory, I will first concentrate on providing stories of isolated cases of empires that built systems underpinned by philosophies and values independent of European influences.

Knowledge of African territories outside of Egypt only began to filter to Europe after the rise of Islam in North Africa and southern Spain. During the 700 years (711- 1492) of the Islamic empire in Spain, scholarship in Sciences, Architecture and the arts blossomed. At this time, the great West African empires of Ghana and Mali began to take shape. Muslim and Arab scholars not only wrote about the glories of Egypt and Spain, but also about the great West African empires of Ghana, Mali and Songhai. These lands were rich in Gold and other valuable tropical products and the city of Timbuktu was recognised as a centre of Islamic learning from the 13th to the 17th Centuries. It is estimated that up to 700,000 manuscripts of Timbuktu's scholastic heritage survive in public libraries and private collections. They include books on religion, law, literature and science. Timbuktu was added to the UNESCO world heritage list in 1988 for its three mosques and 16 cemeteries and mausoleums. These Monuments, the oldest dates from 1329, played a major role in spreading Islam in West Africa. In 2011, the invading Islamists seeking to overthrow the secular government of Mali destroyed some of the mausoleums after seizing the city. Professor Ali Mazrui describes the glories of Timbuktu as part of a dual legacy in Africa (Africanity and Islam), which led to the recognition of the Malian King Mansa Musa's pilgrimage to Mecca as one of the most glorious events of the last Millennium.

However, away from these major ancient centres known to the outside world such as Timbuktu, little was known of several other empires such as Yoruba (Nigeria), Dagomba-Mossi (Ghana, Burkina Faso, Ivory Coast and Togo), Zimbabwe, Zulu, and the Haya people who live on the shores of Lake Victoria in Tanzania. This ignorance led to many misconceptions about the rest of Africa. For example, as recently as 2009, Jarle Simensen wrote that the use of iron tools came to sub-Saharan Africa later than to other parts of the world; indeed some have talked of a "1000-year lag". Such sweeping conclusions have been the popular narrative about Africa for hundreds of years. However, many of these narratives are now known to be completely out of line with the reality of Africa's past. Thanks to contemporary research, it has been shown that Africa was a leader in iron technology and far more developed in many other areas of early human technological and social development.

Evidence to the contrary

Indeed, recent research findings continue to accentuate the fact that the pioneering achievement of a Neolithic agricultural civilization in Africa dates back 7,000 years and the use of iron has now been found to date back to about 1200 BC. Professor Roderick J. McIntosh of the Department of Anthropology at Rice University wrote in the Journal of the Archaeological Institute of America in 1999 that archaeologists long thought that agriculture must always have preceded herding in Africa, and that the idea of plant domestication was imported from the Near East around the turn of the third millennium B.C. However, in the last two decades, research has shown that experiments with sorghum and millet began as early as 9,000 years ago, and full domestication happened as early as 900 B.C. Furthermore, iron furnaces have been found dating from the eighth century B.C., and possibly as early as 1300 B.C.; true steel was invented by the middle of the first millennium B.C.

In the Film "The Tree of Iron" Professor Peter Schmidt documents archaeological work on ancient civilizations of the Haya people in Tanzania and their traditional iron smelting process. Two decades of study in the region by Schmidt, an archaeologist and historian has revealed ancient, 2000 year old iron industrial sites, as well as extensive oral traditions that illustrate the role of iron in agriculture, political power, and mythology. It presents convincing evidence of early indigenous technologies far more complex than previously thought. The Tree of Iron is set in Tanzania, East Africa, on the western shores of Lake Victoria, where Haya people have lived for centuries. Schmidt's work with African iron smelters who build and operate reconstructed versions of traditional iron smelting furnaces, demonstrates the technological principles that the ancients also used to obtain high furnace temperatures and to produce high carbon steel. It also illustrates the degradation of the environment caused by this ancient industry.

In West Africa, iron smelting among the Yoruba, Hausa, Bassari and Dagomba peoples was common centuries before European contact. The Yoruba mastered iron and Brass smelting over hundreds of years and the Bassari iron smelting industry was a main supplier of

11

iron to Dagomba farmers and warriors as far back as the 15th century. Further, the existence of these states with systems of government that allowed for peaceful development of durable cultural traditions, artifacts and agriculture debunks the European held view of Africa as a land of savages.

The Dagomba-Mossi States (from 13th Century)

Although much has been written about the great West African empires, very little is known about the Dagomba-Mossi states, which began in the 13th century. These states, which I will refer to as The Mamprusi-Dagomba-Mossi states consist of sister empires of Mamprusi, Dagomba, Nanumba (in today's Ghana), and Mossi (in Burkina Faso, Ivory Coast) and other Mole-Dagbani groups such as the Dagaba. These states were founded by Naa Gbewa and his children in about 1300 AD, having begun in the second half of the 1200s. They constitute one of few empires in Africa that have been in continuous existence, almost unaltered for nearly 700 years. These empires provided stable systems of government long before the first Portuguese (European) fleet visited what was to be known later as the Gold Coast in 1471. In fact they were established for about 350 years before later kingdoms such as Ashanti came into existence.

At the zenith of their power, the Mamprusi-Dagomba-Mossi states controlled almost all of northern Ghana, and northeast Cote D'Ivoire and the entire Burkina Faso into the Macina area of Mali. According to Illiasu (1971), during their second northern expansion the Mossi-Dagomba states reached eastern Macina and Lake Debo in ca.1400, Benka in ca. 1433 and Walata in 1477-83 (all in present-day Mali). The son of a Dagomba prince called Bounkani created the Kingdom of Bouna in Cote D'Ivoire. The Oyoko ruling clan of Ashanti traces its ancestry to the Dagomba ruled Kingdom of Bouna. Some historians have said that the Mamprusi-Dagomba-Mossi states succeeded the empires of Old Ghana and Mali. And what is worth noting is that the Mamprusi-Dagomba-Mossi empires continue to this day to observe the same political systems, established nearly 700 years ago, in which several layers of chiefs look up to the king at the apex. This is still true of the Mossi, Mamprusi, Dagomba, Nanumba and other Mole-Dagbani groups.

Apart from controlling large areas of land, the Mamprusi-Dagomba-Mossi society was organised around a clan system based on different occupations or trades and children from each clan specialised in the occupation or trade of their clan. The clans included Kings, Barbers,

Butchers, Blacksmiths, Drummers, Landowners & Earth priests, Warriors, Weavers (of clothes), Cobblers, Hunters, etc. Children had to work hard to learn the clan hierarchies, trade, dance and the meaning of the clan music. It was a disgrace not to know all these and therefore children strove to be the best in their entire clans. The drumming and music practices became entrenched and sophisticated in the Dagomba state in a unique and interesting way; namely drumming as a medium of recording history.

Drumming and Music for Recording History

One of the unique and sophisticated aspects of the Dagomba tradition was keeping a comprehensive oral history through drums and music. In the absence of widespread use of written language, the Dagomba-Mamprusi-Mossi peoples preserved their history in drum and music. In the Dagomba state for example, the drum history provides details of ascension to the kingship (called Ya-Naa) for over 40 kings. The drummers called Lunsi descend from Bizung a one of sons of the Dagomba King, Naa Nyagsi (1416-1432).

List of Dagomba Kings as reported from Dagomba Drum /Music History

1. Tohazie (and group invader hunters arrive in Northern Ghana and southern Burkina Faso (ca 1250-60)

2. Kpugnumbo (Son of Tohazie and the princess of the Mali King) becomes Chief of Biung (ca 1300)

3. Naa Gbewa (Son of Kpugnumbo) First King of Greater Dagomba or Dagbon - ca 1320-1365)

4. Naa Zirli (First Son of Na Gbewa) –Rules greater Dagbon or Dagomba (ca 1365- 1375)

5. Naa Tohagu (3rd Son of Naa Gbewa) -Moved greater Dagbon capital from Pusiga to Gambaga in ca 1378) *The Grandson of Naa Gbewa by his only daughter Princess Yanienga creates the Mossi States*

6. Naa Sitobu (Youngest son of Naa Gbewa - Establishes new Dagomba (1384 -1414)

7. Naa Nyagsi (Son of Naa Sitobu) (1415-1432) - *Built new Capital at Diari*

8. Naa Zulandi (1432 to 1442)

9. Naa Bierigudeera (1442 to 1454)

23. Naa Andani I - Sigli (1677 to 1687)

24. Naa Binbiegu (1687 to 1700)

25. Naa Gariba (1700 to 1720)

26. Naa Nasalan Ziblim (1720 to 1735)

27. Naa Ziblim (1735 to 1740)

28. Naa Ziblim Kulunku (1740 to 1760)

29. Naa Andani II –Jangbariga (1760 to 1778)

30. Naa Suman Zoli (1778 to 1799)

31. Naa Yakubu 1 (1799-1839)

13

10. Naa Darigudeera (1454 to 1469) (His son marries the daughter of a local chief of Bouna in Ivory Coast and their male offspring called Bounkani establishes the famous Bouna Kingdom).

11. Naa Zolgu (1469 to 1486)

12. Naa Zongma (1486 to 1506)

13. Naa Ningmitooni (1506 to 1514)

14. Naa Dimani (1514 to1527)

15. Naa Yanzoe (1527 to 1543)

16. Naa Darizegu (1543 to 1554)

17. Naa Luro (1554 to 1570)

18. Naa Titugri (1570 to 1589)

19. Naa Zagli (1589 to 1608)

20. Naa Zokuli (1609 to 1627)

21. Naa Gungobili (1627 to 1648)

22. Naa Zanglna (1648 to 1077)

32. Naa Abdulai I (1864-1876)

33. Naa Andani II (1876-1899)

34. Naa Darimani (1899-1899)

35. Naa Alasani (1899 -1917)

36. Naa Bukari Andani (1920-1920 – abdicated)

37. Naa Abdulai II 1917-1938 (Regent 1917-1920, after Naa Bukari's abdication ruled from 1920 to 1938)

38. Naa Mahama II (1938-1948)

39. Naa Mahama III (1948-1953)

40. Naa Abdulai III (1953-1967)

41. Naa Andani III (1968-1969)

42. Naa Mahamadu Abdulai (1970-1974)

43. Naa Yakubu Andani (1974 -)

According to the oral tradition, the first drummer was Bizung, a son of Naa Nyagsi whose mother died very early, sealing his fate to a life of suffering and neglect in the king's household. He did not have motherly care or enough to eat and had worn out clothing. He was often teased by the other children and found comfort in drumming on a calabash drum. He soon perfected his drumming and music using it to praise past kings as well as express his dissatisfaction with daily issues. He was soon recognised by his father, Naa Nyagsi and offered a paramount chieftaincy position. Bizung declined and instead his father appointed him as the court historian; decreeing that the drummer role was to carry respect from all kings. Thus the role of the drummer in Dagomba state was created. All drummers descend from Bizung, are considered royalty and have a hierarchical system of chieftaincy that parallels the royal one. The drummer families can be found in all four tribes that descend from Naa Gbewa.

In Dagomba (appropriately called Dagbon) the drummers are both entertainers and historians of the Dagomba people. Abdulai Salifu in his work *Names that Prick: Royal Praise Names in Dagbon, Northern Ghana* wrote: "The drummers' craft is both an economic endeavour and a cultural responsibility...their art meets economic needs and they also serve as living archives and the collective memory of the populace (p. 86). Christine Oppong (1973: 54) also observed that the drummers (*lunsi*) in Dagbon are court historians and musicians and their unbroken historical narratives are very vital to the continuity of the traditional system. These drummers/praise singers are found at all social events, and at royal courts.

At a special annual event called Sambanlunga, knowledgeable oral historians weave together intriguing narratives about the kings of Dagbon, their bravery, stewardship and achievements. This event often spans a number of evenings and takes a deep look into the history of Dagbon. The Sambanlunga is an educational and commemorative event. Young drummers rehearse and renew their knowledge of the history and the ordinary people are reminded of the glories of their forefathers. The sambanlunga reminds people of their familial connections, tracing their roots back to important figures in their past and hearing the praise-names of an important ancestor.

Abdulai Salifu puts this more eloquently saying that:

The praise names the drummers sing or use to address their patrons at ceremonies are abridged historical mythic narratives, taken from the myths and legends of the Dagbamba. The narration assumes mythical dimensions and religious beliefs and practices are woven into the telling of the tale" .... *Their praise poetry rekindles in their patrons that sense of belonging to a rich cultural system that transcends time. The present is what it is because it has a link with an antecedent time. Dagomba praises thus encode history, just as much as they offer commentaries on political figures. Each praise epithet has a history, and depending on the situation, a short praise epithet can be expanded into hours of narrative text that evoke the myths and legends of the ethnic group (p.89).*

The Dagomba also developed clan music for more than 14 different clan groups organized around professions and trades: Kings/chiefs, Butchers, Barbers, Drummers, Blacksmiths, Fiddlers, Warriors, Weavers, Builders, Hunters, etc. Clan music and dances are attached to the sense of identity and individuals must learn to dance to the tunes from their fathers' and mothers' clans. The unique value of the Dagomba drummers' work and traditions is not only that it recorded the history of the kingdom but also the histories of its neighbours.

Many accounts about the rulers of neighbouring kingdoms such as Gonja, Ashanti and the Konkomba, which are written today, come from such drum histories. The Dagomba drummers' craft and skills are renowned and several US universities today teach Dagomba drumming.

Another important aspect of the traditions of the Mamprusi-Dagomba-Mossi states is the development of a universal guiding principle of living embodied in two words: *Bilchini* or *Burkini* /*Burkina* and *Behagu*. The principle of Bilchini (in Dagomba Mamprusi languages) or Burkini /Burkina (in the Mossi language from which the name Burkina Faso is derived) denote honesty and integrity. The name Burkina Faso means the land of people with honesty and integrity or "the land of upright people". The two words are taken from the major native languages of Burkina Faso -Moore and Dioula, respectively. Figuratively, "Burkina" may be translated, as "men of integrity", and "Faso" means "fatherland" in Dioula.

As a guiding philosophy, the Mamprusi-Dagomba-Mossi traditions of honesty in inter-dealings and maintaining integrity in your conduct were essential qualities of being a member of the group. This was held in high esteem, and so there is a common saying among these three related traditions which is always expressed when a person fails the test of honesty and integrity. It simply states, "O ka bilchinsi", which means, "He has no honesty and integrity".

Behagu is a loaded concept encompassing many values around inter-dealings and responsibility for others. The Dagomba-Mossi tradition denoted a sense that a person had to be responsible, to strive for community good and solidarise with other people as a way of making himself, his family and community an example for others. Therefore strangers are to be taken care of and included as much as possible in the family and community. For reason of demonstrating Behagu to strangers it was common in the Dagomba-Mossi tradition that families could dip into their stock of grains, reserved for planting in the new farming season to provide food for strangers. This extreme determination to show Behagu culminated in the proverb, which states that "The stranger has no way of knowing that the dinner provided to him has been prepared from your sorghum seeds, and you must keep it that way". To do otherwise is to show that you did not have behagu.

The Yoruba

One of the well-known old and great West African empires is the Yoruba. The Yoruba state is at least 1000 years old. In his book titled "Ile-Ife-The Source of Yoruba Civilisation", Prince Adelegan Adegbola said that "the Yorubas are the progeny of great kingship, efficient kingdom-builders and astute rulers. They have been enjoying for centuries a well-organised and refined political and social system. The Yoruba people trace their ancestry to the black Cushite who migrated from the Middle East. More specifically, oral narratives from Oyo say that the people left the area of present day Mecca, under the leadership of Oduduwa around 600 BCE. They settled first near the banks of the River Nile where they intermingled with the tribes of the Nile valley such as the Nubians. They eventually migrated to what is now known as the Northeastern zone of Nigeria and once again mingled and bred with the Kanuris of the Borno area and other local tribes. From there they eventually migrated down south to the forests and farm lands of what is now known as south-western Nigeria making their primary place and location of settlement and pagan worship. Ile-Ife is the centre of Yoruba from where the sons of their great ancestor Oduduwa moved out to establish their own independent Yoruba kingdoms, which are spread out across South-eastern Nigeria today. Some of the kingdoms such the Oyo Empire became powerful and successful and contributed to the shaping of the destiny and future of the large kingdom. Oyo, in particular is credited with putting an end to the advance of the jihad of Usman Dan Fodio towards the coastal communities of the Yoruba kingdom.

In southern Africa, the famous empire of Great Zimbabwe (1250 and 1550) and the Zulu empire are examples of African kingdoms that exercised great power before European colonisation. Empires such as Ashanti rose after the arrival of Europeans on the African coast and in her 200 years of growth and glory, Ashanti demonstrated that African nations were capable developing complex and sustainable social systems. The British curtailed Ashanti power in the war of 1874.

Afrocentrism defends Africa

What I have been trying to portray about Africa here is nothing new and it is what Professor Ali Mazrui calls romantic gloriana. Mazrui says that:

"African scholars, as defense against European arrogance, have sought to emphasize that Africa before the Europeans' arrival had its own complex civilizations of the kind that Europeans regarded as valid and important—civilizations that produced great kings, impressive empires, and elaborate technological skills... It celebrates Africa's more complex achievements. It salutes the pyramids of Egypt, the towering structures of Aksum, the sunken churches of Lalibela, the brooding majesty of Great Zimbabwe, the castles of Gonder. Romantic gloriana is a tribute to Africa's empires and kingdoms, Africa's inventors and discoverers, great Shaka Zulu rather than the unknown peasant. This form of Pan-African cultural nationalism is partially correct; where idealized paradigms combine mythology with real facts attempt to re-invent Africa" (p.77).

In pursing this line of Pan-African cultural nationalist defense, some writers have advanced the argument that the Greeks plagiarized African and Egyptian philosophy and knowledge and made it their own. Among such writers are George G James, Henry Olela, Cheick Anta Diop and Martin Bernal who champion the theory of stolen legacy. The story of stolen legacy began with the work of George G. James, a professor at the University of Arkansas. The book titled Stolen Legacy: Greek Philosophy is Stolen Egyptian Philosophy was published in New York by the Philosophical Library in 1954. The Journal of Pan-African Studies has made the book into an eBook and from this source I quote the George James ideas about the stolen legacy.

In chapter one of his book, George James writes that Pythagoras received his training in Egypt, and returned to his native island, Samos, where he established his order. He later migrated to Croton (540 B.C.) in Southern Italy, and witnessed it grow enormously before his expulsion. George James then makes the case that several Greek philosophers, like Pythagoras studied in Egypt and went back to propagate their knowledge in Greece. He cites the cases of Thales (640 B.C.) and his associates Anaximander and several other natives from Ionia in Asia Minor, which was a stronghold of the Egyptian Mystery schools. These include Anaximenes, Xenophanes (576 B.C.), Parmenides, Zeno and Melissus, Heraclitus (530 B.C.),

Empedocles, Anaxagoras and Democritus who were also natives of Ionia interested in physics. He then concludes that while Egypt was familiar with and adored philosophy, the Greeks were not and this explained why the Athenians sentenced Socrates to death in 399 B.C. and also caused Plato and Aristotle to flee for their lives from Athens. His arguments point to African antiquity, the Greeks as plagiarist of African knowledge and of Africa as important in the history of human civilization.

These ideas have been taken over by other writers such as Henry Olela, Cheick Anta Diop, and Martin Bernal. Such writers all strive to accentuate the idea of holding Africa and Egypt in particular as the legitimate origin of Western thought. However, Martin Bernal in his book *Black Athena* argues that these distortions were not made by ancient Greeks but modern Europeans who on entering a new era of racism and anti-Semitism, (in the words of Ali Mazrui), could not make themselves bear the thought that what they regarded as the pristine origins of their civilization should have had much to do with either Africans or such Semitic peoples as the Phoenicians. Modern Europeans, therefore, promptly understressed, if not "obliterated," Egypt's contribution to Athens" (p.78).

Tunde Adeleke in his work "*The Case Against Afrocentrism*" writes that Afrocentric scholars such as Molefi Asante, Marimba Ani, Maulana Na'im Akbar, Karenga and John Henrik Clark focus on proving three key facts: the antiquity of history and civilization in Africa, the superiority and influence of African civilization over European, and the universality of the African Worldview" (p.90). Amos Wilson is said to have argued that this approach would allow black people to try to take back what European histography has stolen and completely falsified, while also erasing the new false identities it placed on African Egyptian people. In this way they replace Eurocentric diffusionist's theory with an Afrocentric one.

In his article titled African thought: Did the Greek's plagiarize our philosophy?" Nzau wa Musau writes that in spite of Socrates admitting that he studied philosophy and medicine in Egypt and the fact that Egyptians practiced medicine and inspired the earliest known medical books such as the Hearst Papyrus (7th dynasty, 2000BC) and the Kahun Papyrus (12th & 13th dynasty, 2133-1766BC), the stolen legacy theory succeeds in merely inferring existence of philosophy in Africa and not in essentially proving it. He concludes that

"Much more work needs to be done to prove the practice of philosophy in antiquity Africa and before the alleged Greek theft or plagiarism. If philosophy is to be proven in Africa, it is not to be sought in Europe but through undivided philosophical examination of African ways, systems, beliefs, history, cultures and reasoning. Stolen or not stolen, the evidence of practice of philosophy in Africa should be very apparent even in the present if indeed it was there. If it's not, a lot of questions arise" Para 13).

Professor Ali Mazrui makes an evolutionary argument, stating that the recent recognition of Africa as the origin of man illustrates the fact that Africa created the Human social systems such as the Family and is therefore, the cradle of other social systems of human kind.

The problem with Afrocentrism

Tunde Adeleke observes that the problem with Afrocentrism is its ethnocentric and cultural jingoistic overtone, which in order to enhance black self-esteem advanced a "monolithic construction of black Diaspora identity; a romantised view of the African past (pre European) a past of harmony, and advanced cultural and civilizational achievements. They depict Africa as a continent inhabited by people who are morally and ethically superior to all others" (p.91). Yaacov Shavit in his work *History in Black. African-Americans in Search of an Ancient Past* observes that the desire of Afrocentric mythology was a desire for antiquity to establish originality and distinctiveness, a desire, which is driven by the denial of African antiquity. To Shavit, a claim to antiquity is an important tool in a vanquished nation's struggle for pride, dignity and status (in Tunde, p.92).

To a large extent Yaacov Shavit seems to dismiss the benefits of antiquity. However, the fight for recognition of a personal legacy mistakenly or unjustifiably denied is an essential part of the human spirit. For Africans to abandon that fight would in itself be indicative of a lack of that human spirit. Afrocentrists therefore are justified to fight for that legacy and although their conclusions are quite inspiring about Africa's past, they do not answer the critical questions of Africa's present. The intent of this book is about Africa's present and future and in this regard, whether or not Africa had a glorious past, the important questions to ask are: What happened to Africa after that glorious period? Why did Africa stagnate and Europe progress? What is Africa doing today?

20

Chapter 3
Africa's Stagnation: Popular and Alternative Explanations

The question of what went wrong in Africa has been asked over and over again. Commentators, researchers and critics of Africa's underdevelopment have attributed it to the debilitating effects of slavery and colonialism to current international political and economic structures, which marginalise poor African countries. Writers who focus on the latter have argued that development work has been 'imperialistic and either dismissive or ignorant of the unique realities of non-western nations such as African societies. Jonathan Nunn in a 2002 article *the legacy of Colonialism: A Model of Africa's underdevelopment* concluded that: Africa's continued economic stagnation has to do with colonialism, which continues to have, a persistent impact on economic development. The past effects of extraction are still felt, because the society has been permanently moved to a new equilibrium characterized by high levels of corruption, rent-seeking and insecure property rights. This is the legacy of colonialism. Here, the woes of Africa are seen in economic terms and the causes are more external to Africa.

Many others have held that these historical events alone do not completely explain the African predicament and secondly that any attempt at a monolithic and unifying discourse about Africa is too simplistic. Firstly, if oppression is supposed to be the root cause of underdevelopment, then it is important to note that the impact of colonialism in many parts of Africa was not different from Asia. Secondly, given that African populations have been free of direct colonial control for the last 50 years, some internal factors have been canvassed as reasons for the stagnation. In line with this, internal factors such as geographic and demographic conditions have been advanced as key factors in Africa's development stagnation. The internal arguments appear persuasive for two reasons. First, African countries have been free to determine their destinies for half a century and secondly, the effects of slavery and colour discrimination are less severe in Africa in comparison to the ongoing experiences of African Americans, who live in conditions that (in the words of Bulhan, 1985) impose on them a measure of marginality and alienation. Thus, after 50 years of self-determination, it will be fair to say that the prevailing unpleasant living conditions and development stagnation are in some ways self-imposed; deriving from the chosen paths and actions of the African nations and societies. These chosen paths, I argue, are more at the heart of the African condition today. Jonathan Nunn's analogy for example identifies corruption, rent seeking and insecure property rights, as factors contributing to African underdevelopment, but Nunn fails to link these factors to contemporary values, which constitute the enduring fabric of every society upon which the society builds the future.

For me, a more specific question is: Why did Africa not progress from the stage where she had mastered iron technology? Undoubtedly, there is some value in the role of slavery and colonial exploitation in Africa's the stagnation. The expansion of the slave trade robbed Africa of large numbers of quality human capital and stagnated thinking, creativity, and economic production. However, internal causative factors historically and today are much to blame. Jarle Simensen in a 2009 article mentioned that Geographical and demographic conditions are key factors in Africa's limited development. In particular, that fact that the use of iron tools came to sub-Saharan Africa later than to other parts of the world; the lack of written traditions; the continent being unsuitable for agriculture; the existence of indigenous diseases that afflict both humans and animals; low density of population; continuous migration and settlement in new areas and few tightly-knit, stable settlements with established social structures that could form the basis for enduring states and empires of the kind that have fostered advanced civilisations in other parts of the world. Many of these factors are not wholly true but have been shaped over time into facts. I believe that the some of Simensen's causative factors, which are part of the popular explanations, need to be challenged by providing alternative explanations. .

Alternative Views About Lack of Progress in Africa

There are three of Simensen's causative factors that require attention. They are the late use of iron in Africa, the harsh geography and climate and the absence of stable settlements and the role of written tradition. The first point has already been proven to be wrong because the use of iron began in Africa much earlier than in some other parts of Europe. The other factors have been explained in very simplistic terms and fail to get to the heart of the issues. For this

22

reason I take a different view about the role of geography and climate and argue that African climate is rather predictable and stifles creativity.

The Role of Africa's Predictable Climate on Creative Thinking

The role of climate in Africa's development has been linked to agricultural development, with many writers looking at it in terms of the effect of a harsh climate on agriculture. However, I see the effect of climate on development more in terms of its predictability. In Africa, the sun rises and sets in a predictable fashion and has not changed for millennia. Much of sub-Saharan-Africa has a predictable tropical climate characterised by wet and dry seasons. These two seasons can be predicted almost 100% of the time for decades, unless there is drought. This predictability over several thousands of years meant that many African societies did not have to strive beyond a certain limit to make a living out of their natural environment. There were no extremes of cold and weather changes that could not be overcome by patchy clothing, a simple hut for shelter or taking sheltering under the shade of trees. Additionally, a variety of fruits, food and edible leaves could be harvested or grown for sustenance with minimal hardship, exertion of energy or cognitive activity, nearly all year round, except in the desert areas. For these reasons the African populations were not severely challenged by extreme, intense or constant environmental variations.

In colder climates, the cold weather can be unforgiving and the intensity of the weather, highly unpredictable. While warm weather makes people want to do more physically active tasks, cold weather forces people to sit and think critically about their surroundings and how to tame it. Historically, humans who lived in cold climates had to figure out more sophisticated ways of overcoming the cold and dealing with the unpredictable intensities of the weather. Thousands of years of disasters and the cumulative experiences of their ancestors pushed them towards more creative ways of dealing with their harsh environments and through this incessant drive, they extended their creative capacities and values.

The hypothesis that challenging physical environments are correlated with high levels of creative thinking can be seen when we compare peoples of the temperate climates (which are harsh and unforgiving) with those in warmer climates, which are quite mild and more predictable. Creative thinking resides in the cognitive

23

processes of all human kind, but it is nurtured by the challenges of the environment. Human populations, in warmer climates of Africa, Asia and Latin America have been overwhelmingly dependent on nature's providence and therefore have not vigorously pursued huge changes to our immediate natural environments beyond subsistence agriculture. I believe that predictability is a huge barrier to creative development and from a cognitive and behavioural perspective creative development in Africa and other warmer climates has been tamed by the more predictable climate, which has not challenged our populations enough to extend our cognitive boundaries.

In line with the above, I am of the opinion that creative thinking in historical Africa was tamed immediately after our great ancestors mastered iron smelting and developed agriculture, including irrigation in the great Nile Valley of Ethiopia, Sudan and Egypt. From then onwards we seem to have developed a tamed creative thinking culture, due in part to complacency. This seemingly tamed creative thinking culture has somehow endured in both our individual thinking and societal values, which are more rooted in tradition rather than change. For example traditional technologies around charcoal making, developed thousands of years ago, have hardly changed in Africa. Indeed, we in Africa love tradition because it is a positive philosophy that guarantees stability, continuity and identity. However in a world of dynamic change, an extreme inclination towards tradition will spell stagnation. Thus when one analyses this hypothesis about the role of predictable climate and tradition in creative thinking, one would realise that from about 7,000 BC when the populations of Africa mastered iron to make simple tools for hunting and farming, they had conquered the biggest obstacles to survival. And for this reason perhaps they did not find the need to strive for other things. In other words, their ability to provide shelter and grow food to supplement natural food sources, marked the end of an urgent motivation to push cognitive processes in other sophisticated ways. In such a scenario, any urgent need to extend the cognitive process would have had to be precipitated by a new and catastrophic change in the environment. Luckily, this did not happen; the sun rose and set in the same predictable fashion, giving rise to the wet and dry seasons that have hardly changed for millennia. Thus, in comparison to our cousins who moved into semi-temperate and temperate regions of Europe and northern Asia, who were challenged by the harsh and unforgiving climatic environments, African populations were less challenged. Today it is still common to see that only half of the 12-

hour day, the morning and late afternoons, are suited for work. In the heat of the African day, people are sitting under the shade of trees to cool off, relax and play games. It is less about work. The night is still too warm for serious thinking and in most cases it is pitch dark unless it is full moon and so people have to go to sleep. This is so predictable all year round and has been like this for millennia.

Lack of Large and Enduring Empires and Africa's Development

Simensen made a sweeping conclusion that the lack of stable settlements hindered development in Africa and I find that rather simplistic. To me it is not the lack of settlements but the lack of large and enduring empires. It is important to remember as Simensen acknowledges that African history was not devoid of political dynamism and that progressive medieval kingdoms existed in West and Eastern Africa for millennia and before European contact. However, Africa stands apart from the Middle East, Asia, and Europe in the sense that there were no extensive empires similar to the Persian or Roman empires that cemented together large populations across thousands of miles for extensive periods or for several centuries. Most empires were smaller and lasted on a few hundred years, often not long enough to live enduring values and systems. Thus when it comes to comparing Africa to Europe and Asia, the differences lie in the historical absence of broad, common and extensive cultural experiences associated with large empires across the African continent.

Historically, large and enduring empires such as the Greek, Egyptian, Roman, Persian, Chinese, Japanese and later Islamic, had the profound effect of bringing together values and technologies of smaller minority groups and distilling them into a coherent set of beliefs, processes and skills that advanced the quality of the lives of their populations. For example, at the zenith of its power, the Persian Empire could boast of advanced technology in several areas of human endeavour including architecture, literature and the arts. The same could be said of the Greeks, Egyptians, Chinese and the Islamic Empires. Such advancement in human values and technological knowledge came to a head in Islamic Spain and laid the foundation for the industrial revolution in Europe. Africa south of the Sahara did not have such large and enduring empires until about 1100 AD. But those powerful and relatively extensive empires such as Ghana, Mali and Songhai did not last beyond 150 years and were often unstable because of the constant raids from more stable

25

Islamic states of North Africa. Thus instead of advancing and maintaining trade links, the North African empires contributed to the demise of the large West African empires. These developments reduced the potential for these empires to spread the distilled knowledge and values of diverse populations to other areas over long periods of time, in order to exert a lasting and transformative effect on other areas of Africa. On the other hand, in much of Asia and Europe, the positive effects of living as part of large empires over several generations, were that large sections of people came to develop much more broad and similar understandings of the philosophies of living. In this way, they created near homogeneous sets of values and ways of living across vast geographic areas and language groups. These became the strong foundations for developing pride in their unique traditional philosophies and cultures, including an extreme, yet positive value around the need to achieve mastery in all domains of human endeavour. To my mind, large empires promoted competition, new discoveries and the development of new technologies. They also fostered the need for specialisation and mastery of skills. Herein lies the disadvantage of the lack of enduring empires in Africa. Indeed what transpired was a situation where small enclaves of African groups developed and kept their own values and technologies, both good and bad for hundreds of years with little or no renewal. The lack of real contact and experience with the cultural dynamism associated with vast empires elsewhere outside Africa meant that at the threshold of European colonialism, many African tribes experienced very little change and their contact with new European religious beliefs, ways of thinking and technologies was profoundly astounding. This created in many quarters, a strong affective intoxication and gullibility that led to the near complete abandonment of traditional ways of thinking and doing.

Written Traditions and Development

Simensen and some other authors have argued that the lack of written tradition that is characteristic of large and enduring empires is one of the reasons for limited progress in Africa. Although that has some merit, I argue that written traditions many African Empires in East Africa (Egypt, Abyssinia) and West Africa (Ghana, Mali, Songhai) had written traditions. I argue further that written traditions are not the only way knowledge and values are transmitted. And there is evidence in most indigenous cultures of traditions being passed on orally from generation to generation. In some cultures this was also done via music. Empires like the Dagomba of northern Ghana have had their oral traditions preserved in drum history and many others preserved their traditions in other oral forms. And since the majority of African populations were stable rather than nomadic, successive generations understood their environments through knowledge passed down from earlier generations.

Black Identity: Legacy of a Constructed Image

Black identity has been constructed through religious interpretations in the Middle East and European-American contact with Africa. This constructed image functioned negatively at several levels-psychological, political, and economic to turn an independent group into subjects of oppression and marginalisation. In the Bible, blackness of the skin is attributed to the story of Ham. Ham's descendants were reportedly cursed and several literary sources affirm the idea that the story of Ham acquired racial interpretations in later years among early Jewish and Christian writers. These suspicious interpretations of the origin of black people were later used in early Judaic teachings and Middle-Eastern (Arab, Jewish) slave merchants, and later Western Christian slave merchants used these interpretations to justify slavery.

An excerpt from the online encyclopedia, Wikipedia refers to these early constructions and quotes the Babylonian Talmud, Sanhedrin 108b thus: "Our Rabbis taught: Three copulated in the ark, and they were all punished—the dog, the raven, and Ham. The dog was doomed to be tied, the raven expectorates [his seed into his mate's mouth], and Ham was smitten in his skin" (Talmud Bavli, Sanhedrin 108). Later commentaries described Ham's "smitten" skin as a darkening of skin and this was also later interpreted as referring to the blackness of Ham's descendants. In line with this, rabbis in the Bereshit Rabbah assert that Ham himself emerged from the ark black-skinned and Zohar (A non-Scriptural book) states that Ham's son Canaan "darkened the faces of mankind"(171).

This version of the origin and status of black people is disputed by a notable medieval Jewish commentator on the Torah, Abraham ibn Ezra. He observes that this version is untrue and that those who argue that the Cushim (descendants of Ham who had black skin) are slaves because Noah was cursed are wrong. According to Abraham Ibn Ezra, King Nimrod, the first king after the flood, was a descendant of Cush and if the curse interpretation was correct, then

27

Nimrod could not have become king but would have remained a slave.

This counter interpretation was known for millennia and yet black people were subjected to all sorts of indignity in the three main religions of the Middle East - Judaism, Christianity and Islam. Even though Christian sources in Africa (Egypt and Ethiopia) mentioned this curse, it was never associated with the notion of black inferiority among the African Coptic Churches in North Africa and Abyssinia. However, sections of Arab-Muslim societies adopted this interpretation both in attitudes and deeds, including the practice of slavery. In fact, the enslavement of black people was widespread in the Middle East before Islam. And although Islam abolished slavery in principle, slavery was widely practised in Islamic countries. Arab slave dealers operated along the North and East Coast of Africa as far as Mozambique. In fact it is still widely practised in the region even in the 21st Century. In relation to this current reality of slavery in the Middle East, Ray Jureidini writing on the subject in 2002 observed that migrant workers with dark skin from the India sub-continent and Africa are subjected to modern day slavery supported by government policies that deny them even the most minimal form of citizenship rights.

European scholars of the Bible in the Middle Ages also took on board these ideas. It gained currency during the slave trade and was used to justify slavery and the exploitation of African slaves. Many Church groups including the Mormon and the Latter-day Saint churches taught that black people were under the curse of Ham and excluded them from the church in many ways. In his book 'Civilization on Trial' Toynbee predicted that future historians would say that 'the great event of the 20th Century was the impact of Western civilization upon all other living societies of the world of that time. And that its impact was so powerful, overwhelming and pervasive that it turned the lives of all its victims upside down and inside out, affecting every domain of their lives. For Africa this impact did not begin in the 20th century, but with the European powers' first contact with Africa. This was the beginning of the process of turning lives upside down and inside out.

Africa's contact with the west accelerated and accentuated some myths about, and misrepresentations of black people that were held by Middle-eastern and southern European societies. The European hegemonic construction and maintenance of negative black identity derived from the historical discourses about dark-skinned people by

Middle-Eastern monotheistic religious groups or the adherents of Judaism, Christianity and Islam. These beliefs then became entrenched under the trans-Atlantic slave trade. At the core of the construction of otherness is the innate desire to find worth in the self in comparison with others. This tendency is a common psychological trait, which has positive implications for the constructor and negative implications for those that are being compared. The construction of race had these motivations and racism has been at the centre of the Blackman's historical and contemporary tragedy. If racism is regarded as synonymous with race prejudice and discrimination, then it manifests in a set of attitudes toward dark-skinned people. This type of racism is rooted in Ham's supposed curse in the Bible.

Black identity in America and Africa

The peculiar interpretation of Ham's story added to the pseudoscientific theory about race in Europe and America and began the process of constructing the image of "Blackness". It begot slavery and racism, two of the most damaging forms of psychological and physical violence, unleashed by more powerful humans on others in the evolutionary history of Homo sapiens. The scourge of slavery and racism on continental Africa and on the descendants of slaves was and remains an indelible part of the psyche of black populations and many allude to its historical impact on the present.

Walter Rodney, an advocate for the abolition of the slave trade, asserted that commerce between Europe and Africa was the first and decisive step in the underdevelopment of Africa. This commercial relationship forced Africa into what can be called a "colonial" trade in people. It led to the depopulation of Africa and created a structural disequilibrium in the African society. It is estimated that between the years 1701 and 1807 British traders carried approximately 2.5-3.7 million slaves from Africa to various parts of North America. The subjugation and "de-humanisation" of the slaves on the basis of colour in the Americas led to the profound entrenchment of the mechanism of social and economic exclusion based on colour. The fundamental idea that a small group of Caucasian people (slave owners) wielded enough power to determine, in absolute terms, the life outcomes of other people, without the victims having the capacity to challenge their fate, set in motion the affirmation of speculative biological theory of racial superiority. Racism was now grounded and justified not only in reference to the misinterpretation of the Judeo-Christian Scriptures, but by the realities of slavery. George M. Fredrickson notes in his book "The black image in the white mind" that racism, defined as "a rationalized pseudoscientific theory positing the innate and scientific inferiority of non-whites", (p.8) received broad acceptance in American society. Even Thomas Jefferson (3rd US President, who eventually contributed to the notions of freedom), once held such beliefs stating, in relation to Euclid, a great African mathematician that "no negro could comprehend the investigations of Euclid," Simply, Jefferson was suggesting that blacks were, in the words of Nzau wa Musau, "dull, tasteless and anomalous." Notwithstanding the fact that influential people such as Thomas Jefferson believed in the inferiority of black people, it was still resisted by some people in America.

Fredrickson writes that there was disagreement within a narrow consensus for pseudoscientific racism or its equivalent to increase its hold on the American mind and to infect even those whites who resisted its full implications. Thus these conceptions of the black man as sanctioned by God had huge implications on the way the slave was treated and has followed the African into contemporary times. In reference to reality, Franz Fanon wrote: "The disaster of the man of colour lies in fact that he was enslaved". He also wrote "the disaster and inhumanity of the Whiteman lie in the fact that somewhere he has killed man"

While these racial interpretations of the past centuries have been disputed lately, the acceptance of such unsubstantiated interpretations for millennia has entrenched the belief that the black race is inferior and this is yet to be completely shaken. The tragedy of enslavement and its impact on the collective experiences of the descendants of the slaves is still ravaging the black populations across the world. Denise Isom, discussing African American issues in 2007 wrote of the impact of slavery on the black identity in the following words:

Slavery coupled paradigms of race with deeply imbedded sexist ideologies and began the destruction and subsequent re-creation of the Black psyche. A process housed in an emerging American culture marked by the oppressions intimately woven into its very fabric (p.1-2).

During slavery, many slave masters devised ways of controlling slaves and one came up with a method of subjugating slaves, which was extended to the colonial period

Louis Farrakhan gave a speech a few years ago where he narrated the story of a slave dealer called Willie Lynch, which I reproduce here. According to the story, many slave-owners were brutally murdered until Willie Lynch, a slave-owner himself, came to the United States in 1712. Willie Lynch arrived in the then-colony of Virginia from the West Indies. He came there to teach his methods to the other slave-owners. This is what he said in summary:

"Gentlemen, I have here in my bag a full proof method for controlling your Black slaves. This method, if installed correctly, will control the slaves for at least three hundred to a thousand years. My method is simple! I have noticed a number of differences among the slaves. Difference in age, intelligence, size and sex. I take these differences and make them bigger! In other words, I use their differences to pitch them against each other. By doing so, the slaves themselves will remain perpetually in-cooperative with one another. They will continue to pull each other down to our advantage. This method has worked on my modest plantation in the West Indies. Now that you have a list of differences, I shall give you an outline of action. But before that, I shall assure you that distrust is stronger than trust and envy stronger than adulation, respect or admiration. I use fear, distrust and envy for control purposes! The Black slaves, after receiving this indoctrination, shall carry on and will become self-refueling and self-generating for hundreds of years. In other words, the niggers would remain envious, distrustful and fearful of each other for generations to come. They would never see eye to eye on anything, let alone unite." Willie Lynch then proceeded to lecture his audience on how Blacks could remain in a perpetual state of dependency. This is what he said in summary: "The uncivilized female nigger has a tendency to depend on the uncivilized male nigger for protection. This by nature's design! However, her natural tendency can be reversed, and we did. We reversed nature by burning and pulling a civilized nigger apart and bull-whipping the other to the point of death, all in her presence. By her being left alone unprotected, with the protective male image destroyed, the ordeal caused her to move from her psychologically dependent state to a frozen independent state.

In this frozen psychological state of independence, she will raise her male and female offspring in reversed roles. For fear of the young male's life, she will psychologically train him to be mentally weak and dependent, but physically strong. She will also train her female offspring to be psychologically independent, just like herself. What have you got? You've got the nigger woman out front, the nigger man behind and scared." Indeed, Willie Lynch's method didn't disappoint. It proved to be a success. The slave-owners applied it and the British colonialists didn't hesitate to use it.

These techniques and strategies were adopted by slave owners and evolved into both a practical and psychological approach to thinking and dealing with black people. It also permeated the discourse of those with power to construct the image of Africa and the African. And prominent African writers such as Mbembe, incensed by the sheer magnitude of the negative impact of slavery on black Africans have been concerned about how it has been historically possible to remove colonized Africans from the sphere of humanity in order to manipulate them for imperialist ends. The answer to such a question is that the Africans were an integral part of the process of dehumanization. Thus in outlining this historical process it would be dishonest to discount the role of African kingdoms in the slave trade. Indeed the role of West African Kingdoms such as Ashanti, Macina, Dagomba, the Fanti States, and later on Samory Toure in perpetuating slavery is well documented. The Ashanti Kingdom made its wealth from running a huge machinery of coercion of subordinate tribes who contributed slaves in return for guns and protection for 150 years. The British curtailed this slavery machinery when it defeated Ashanti in the war of 1874. Al-Imamy Samory Toure considered a champion of African freedom traded in slaves even after the official banning of slavery and so did the Macina Kingdom, which was in the regions of modern day Mali and northern Guinea.

The collective and cumulative effect of these events is that they forcibly shaped the Blackman's identity in an almost irretrievable way. For African Americans, Joyce West Stevens in her 1997 work noted that, identity is shaped by trying to synthesize coherent meaning systems from three experiences of socialization: (1) mainstream society (Euro-American worldview); (2) a devalued social status (affected by the status convergence of gender and race); and (3) cultural group reference (Afro-American worldview)" (p.148). Denise Isom then highlighted that fact that living in a predominantly white Anglo-Saxon society conveys a message – at all times – of being a minority, whose voice is drowned by the dominant cultural voice of the majority. This has served to perpetuate the inability of African Americans to take control of the definition of their own identity. Isom quotes Du Bois who noted that the Blackman's identity development is a process of "double consciousness," the "peculiar sensation...of always looking at one's self through the eyes of others, of measuring one's soul by the tape of a world that looks on in amused contempt and pity" (Dubois, 1903, 1994: 2). The words of Du Bois are echoed in Fanon's lamentations about the identity and woes of black people in the colonies. For African Americans, identity is so diffused because it is forever entangled in the conscious and unacceptable systemic discrimination and marginalisation experienced in their daily lives, in which being black is also associated with "lack". In fact, the perceptions of contempt and pity are ever present in many accounts of African people's encounters with highly racialized sections of the American society. To function within those social and ideological constraints, African Americans generate their own images of who they need to be in order to navigate the racial and gender charged environment in which they find themselves. This is also true for people of African descent living in Europe and parts of the Caribbean.

The identity of Africans on the mother continent is today tainted with the notion of inferiority but also of poverty, hunger and suffering. It is also shaped by multiple forces of ethnicity, foreign religions (Christianity and Islam), and contemporary philosophies of race, polity and economics. The colonial discourse has proven a difficult thing to shed because the one-sided nature of knowledge generated and disseminated from the West, which sometimes amounts to epistemic violence, continues unabated. To this, Michael LeFlem wrote in his work *"How the West shaped and distorted African history"*: that the inconceivable and arbitrary violence born out of colonial discourse attest to (the fact that), the power of ideas is often just as effective – or perhaps more effective – than brute force or less institutionalized methods.

The world looks on with amusement and pity and Tony Blair's 2001 expression that the state of Africa is a scar on the conscience of the world, echoes the feelings of profound pity, a perception that Africans humbly accept and yet do nothing to change. Trying to shake the stigma created by pseudoscientific beliefs about race inferiority is hard to do when the asymmetry of economic development is steeped against Africa, which struggles to manage poverty and hunger associated with recurrent droughts and general economic stagnation. Any attempt to shake off the stigma of the colonial discourse must involve creative thinking processes that generate not only changes in inner perceptions of unique identity but also thinking about pragmatic ways of lifting the masses of people out of poverty and deprivation. Only then can people feel strong enough to assert positive images of themselves and the desire to help others.

Chapter 4
Re-constructing Black Identity

African Independence and the Civil Rights Movement

The emergence of the Pan-African movement in the 1920s in the footsteps of Marcus Mosiah Garvey's *Return to Africa* drive was a new beginning in re-constructing black identity. The Pan-African Congress was a confederation of Black Americans, West Indians and Africans formed after the First World War. According to Lee Sustar, writing in the *Socialist Worker*, Pan-Africanism was the Black intellectuals' alternative to Garveyism. At a meeting on the sidelines of the Paris Peace Conference after the First World War, the Pan-Africanist Congress petitioned the colonial powers to allow Black self -determination in Africa and called for an end to segregation in the United States. Championed by W.E.B. Du Bois and joined later by George Padmore (from Trinidad and Tobago), Pan-Africanism sought to unite Black liberation struggles in Africa, the Americas and the West Indies. Pan-Africanism was, in the words of Asante Molefi, a political perspective, a political ideology and a social theory, which pursues a confraternity and continuum in the relationship between Africans and African Americans in order to achieve total emancipation. At its centre was the notion of Afrocentrism, which held the view that black people have always been and were capable of determining their own destiny.

By the 1950s and early 1960s the message of Pan-Africanism was running hand in hand with other Black Nationalist movements such as the Black Muslims Movement (Nation of Islam) which gained prominence when boxing greatest, Muhammad Ali joined their fold. While Pan-Africanism had a much broader influence extending to Africa, the Nation of Islam was more limited to the Americas. The "Nation of Islam" led by Elijah Muhammad preached black uniqueness and the cultivation of pride in black people. Using strong affirmative language, prominent figures of the movement including Malcolm X, Louis Farrakhan and Mohammed Ali, asked black people to stand up for themselves and to endeavour to reconstruct mental processes that allowed them to shake off the yoke of past psychological oppression. They also based their teaching on verses from the Quran. For example, basing their argument on a Quranic verse (Chapter 23:12), which states that God created Adam from black earth (loam), they taught that the first man was a black man. They reasoned that loam, which is the best soil for growing most crops, is made up of soils with different colours and therefore people of different colours came out of the black man. The movement wanted complete separation of Black people from White people. Thus, while their message was important for reconstructing black identity, its extreme exclusionary approach did not make it appealing to some black people.

On the other hand Pan-Africanism, together with Afrocentrism was based on the idea that black people were capable, just as white people, to determine their own destiny. Afrocentrism was viewed as the social expression of the Pan-African ideology, which was, in the words of Tunde Adeleke, to bring fruition to the collective consciousness so that black people become committed to the fight against the constant assault on their humanity and also become aware of their collective destiny. It was therefore more appealing to many people.

The Pan-African philosophical view nursed by people like W.E.B. du Bois and George Padmore came to fruition at some level in the times of Martin Luther King Jr, Kwame Nkrumah and other African independence leaders. George Padmore who headed the International African Service Bureau believed that Pan-Africanism "came of age," following the Fifth Pan-Africanist Congress held in October 1945, in Manchester, England. It was at this meeting that two potential leaders of African independence in the persons of Kwame Nkrumah and Jomo Kenyatta would receive inspiration to liberate their native countries, Ghana and Kenya respectively. Many other African leaders fought for independence with an agenda to use Pan-Africanism as an ideological and political tool that would create broad nationalist feelings as well as a universal brotherhood of people of African descent. On the African continent, Pan-Africanism infused a need for nationalism and this was to be the key ideology not only to free the African people of political dependence but also of economic dependence on the colonialists. Therefore the euphoria of hope and prosperity that came with political independence was effusive.

Padmore wrote in his 1965 book *Pan-Africanism or Communism*:

Here at long last was a philosophy evolved by Black thinkers, which peoples of African descent could claim, and use as their own. The days of dependence on the thinking and direction of their so-called

European friends who had so often betrayed them were over. From henceforth Africans and peoples of African descent would take their destiny into their own hands and march forward under their own banner of Pan-Africanism, in cooperation with their selected allies.

Under this positive picture of black freedom and identity construction, the immediate post-independence era witnessed the coming together of African leaders, black freedom fighters and black artists. As flagged in the introductory chapter, independence for the colony of the Gold Coast (now Ghana) paved the way for the near total liberation of the Africa continent. On 6 March 1957 Ghana became first sub-Saharan African nation to be free from colonialism. It was a testimony to the success of the "Gold Coast Experiment", initiated by the British Government in 1952, to explore the potential of Africans to govern themselves. Kwame Nkrumah became the first Black Prime Minister and led the country to independence. He was determined to see the rest of Africa free and more importantly to chart a new and unique African course, independent of the capitalist West and communist East. This position, he articulated in his famous non-alignment quote: "We face neither East nor West; We face forward".

As an energetic champion of rapid economic growth, Ghana like many African countries pursued rapid educational provision and strong determination to industrialize their economies. Nkrumah's Government built about 600 processing /manufacturing industries in Ghana between 1952 and 1966. It harnessed the power of hydroelectricity of the Akosombo dam in order to drive the new industries. To Kwame Nkrumah, not only was Africa capable of freeing itself of political bondage, but also economic dependency on the West. In his view, a united Africa with one single economic agenda could challenge the entire world because of its huge natural resources. His dream of achieving such a feat was a comprehensive agenda of African unity beginning with the setting of the Organisation of African Unity. A united Africa could give voice to Africa and help redefine the African identity and self-image. Nkrumah urged African leaders during the OAU conference in Addis Ababa in 1963 to forge together in common purpose and policy, in terms of creating a single political, monetary and defense union. He declared:

"If we in Africa can achieve this example of a continent bound together in common purpose and policy, we should have made the finest possible contribution to that peace for which all men and women yearn today. And

this will ease once and forever, the deep shadow of global destruction for mankind. Ethiopia shall stretch forth her hand unto God"

When Nkrumah went for a state visit to the United States in 1958, he used the occasion to remind African-Americans that it was possible to have a black head of state that would be respected by white America. Images of Nkrumah (who, only a few years earlier, was working in a soap factory in New York) in a motorcade driving through Harlem became a magnet and symbol of hope in the possibility of civil rights for people of colour in America. Nkrumah's success in becoming the first leader of an independent sub-Saharan nation fulfilled the dreams of people such as Marcus Garvey, W.E.B de Bois and George Padmore. This motivated du Bois and Padmore to move to Ghana and to broaden the Pan-African movement that saw a clear connection between Africa's freedom movements and those of the Civil Rights Movement in the USA. As more African countries became free in 1960, the mobilization of black peoples against colonization and oppression was gaining momentum in the Caribbean and in the United States of America (USA), where leaders of the Civil Rights campaign emphasised the link between African-American's fight for civil rights and Africa's drive for freedom This propelled black leaders to intensify their fight for equal rights and black reconstruction in the United States.

The connection made by African leaders between Africa's freedom movements and those of the Civil Rights Movement in the USA solidified the Pan-Africanist dimensions of this independence phenomenon. Nkrumah invited Martin Luther King Jr. to Ghana and during this visit King expressed a strong sense that colonialism on the African continent was akin to the injustices against black people in America. It is said that King's visit to Africa was another key moment in the linking of the fight for civil rights in America with freedom for African nations. Lee Suster reports that Dr. King wrote to Black activists, in what was then Southern Rhodesia, and later renamed Zimbabwe, the following words:

Although we are separated by many miles, we are closer together in a mutual struggle for freedom and mutual brotherhood. We realize that injustice anywhere is a threat to justice everywhere. Therefore we are as concerned about the problems in Africa as we are about problems of the United States.

The success of Nkrumah and the independence of African nations underpinned the decision of many young civil rights activists such as Malcolm X and Stokely Carmichael (later Kwame Ture) in the U.S.

to see Black Nationalism as the way forward. Many commentators have observed that Martin Luther King Jr. made explicit this connection on the eve of his assassination in 1968 when he said:

The masses of the people are rising up. And wherever they are assembled today, whether they are in Johannesburg, South Africa; Nairobi, Kenya; Accra, Ghana; New York City; Atlanta, Georgia; Jackson, Mississippi; or Memphis, Tennessee, the cry is always the same: "We want to be free".

Many civil rights leaders visited independent African countries and African heads of state visited the Americas and the Caribbean to make a case for political freedom, equal rights and economic emancipation. One of such important visits was that of Ethiopian Emperor Haile Selassie's visit to Jamaica. It was a visit that electrified the Rastafaris in Jamaica and became a knick-point for the rise of the movement to global prominence. It was also pivotal in propelling the zeal among Rastafaris to fight for black liberation, including the use of Reggae music as a medium of emancipatory expression. Indeed, the Pan-African movement was strengthened beyond the domains of politicians and scholars into the arts, including soul music, hip-hop and later Reggae music. Black artists in various traditions including Funk, Ska/Rocksteady/Reggae and Hip Hop notably, James Brown, Prince Buster, Bob Marley, Jimmy Cliff and Afrika Bambaataa used words of inspiration to progress black positive identity, hope, and spiritual nationalism.

PICTURES: MARCUSS GARVEY, GEORGE PADMORE, DE BOIS, MARTIN LUTHER KING JR. MALCOM X.

African Independence Leaders:
Nkrumah (Ghana),

Jomo Kenyatta (Kenya),

Sekou Toure (Guinea),

Julius Nyerere (Tanzania)

George Padmore
(Leader, Pan-African Movement)

Marcus Garvey
(Back to Africa Movement)

Kwame Nkrumah and Martin
Luther King Jr, in Ghana (1965)

Malcolm X in Africa Source:
Wikipedia

In America, James Brown's famous dictum "Say it loud, I am Black and Proud" was a singular affirmation of self-belief and determination to pursue freedom based on a positive self-image. Analysing the link between Reggae, Hip Hop and Black Nationalism, Ulysses Ronquillo observed: The technical history of the two genres (Hip Hop and Reggae) laid a foundation (serving as an inspiration) for the structural changes that would emerge in American and Caribbean society. The subjugation that the Reggae and Hip Hop communities faced was both race and class-based. Reggae and Hip Hop artists became significant community leaders by drawing on Black Nationalist and Diaspora ideologies to attempt to enter the political realm and reverse the repressive nature of their societies" (para 3). James Brown's "Black and Proud", which epitomized the union between music and the Black Nationalist identity revival is one of those unique songs. In his autobiography James Brown wrote that the song was necessary to teach pride, and I think the song did a lot of good for a lot of people. Although some people called "Black and Proud" militant and angry, James Brown observed that such a view was so because of the line in the song about dying on your feet instead of living on your knees. He also said that he wanted children who heard it to grow up feeling pride in their identity.

Reggae and Pan-Africanism

Reggae, which is synonymous with Jamaica, is music with roots in what was called Ska and Rocksteady. The Ska sound, popular in Jamaica, was transformed into a slower beat that became Rocksteady and later Reggae. In the early 1960s popular singers of Ska included Prince Buster, Aubrey Adams, Desmond Dekker, Duke Reid, King Edwards, Jimmy Cliff, Byron Lee, etc.

Prince Buster, born Cecil Bustamente Campbell, is regarded as one of the most important figures in the history of Ska and Rocksteady music in the 1960s and inspired many reggae musicians. The lyrics of Ska, Rocksteady and Reggae expressed strong Afrocentric and Gaveryism worldview. Prince Buster's music and style in the late 50s reflected Christian fervor intermixed with Afrocentrism that was itself influenced by the Pan-African message and that of the Black Muslim Movement. In his song *Message from the Blackman* Prince Buster emphasised the biological unity of white and black people. And while he laments the treatment of black people in the past, he affirms a new beginning and conviction saying "No matter how hard you try you can't stop me now"

Later, Bob Marley, Toots Hibbert, Jimmy Cliff, Peter Tosh, Burning Spear, and others will take up this message of Afrocentrism and Pan-Africanism.

Even before the rebranding of Jamaican music to Reggae, musicians in Jamaica always sang about oppression, freedom and inequality and the realities of the detached attitudes of those in power about the problems of the poor majority. Politicians were disinterested in what was going on in the lives of the ordinary man. Many Jamaicans realised that the emancipation they envisaged would wipe away all of their troubles, was a mere step in the long struggle towards economic freedom. Yes, political independence was achieved, but many people still lived in poverty. The economic situation was deteriorating and any chance to improve on the wellbeing of the majority of the population was becoming a distant dream.

In this period shortly after independence in 1962, it was apparent that some of the oppression experienced under slavery and colonialism persisted for most Jamaicans. Ulysses notes that Jamaica found racism, social stratification, and an economy on the verge of collapse. One of the songs from Jimmy Cliff, *The Harder They Come* epitomized the dwindling opportunities for earning a living, as the nation's economy got worse. In *The Harder They Come* Cliff lamented the fact that people in power and in the Church were not aware of the everyday suffering of the common people and expected them to wait for their "pie up in the sky". He then states that the people must fight for what is their share and that it is better to fight and die than to live as a puppet or a slave. The broad fight for recognition attained a renewed meaning in the form of the Rastafari religion, at the centre of which was Ethiopian Emperor Haile Selassie. To the Rastafari, Selassie was the God who would deliver them and Reggae provided the spiritual rhythm for their emancipation. The Rastafaris took inspiration from black liberation leaders in the Americas such as Marcus Garvey and De Bois and Ulysses asserts that the Rastafari instituted an intellectual and emotional link between the sufferings under slavery and colonialism and the civil rights and freedom struggles in Africa.

Asante-Darko writing on the theme 'Reggae carrying the message of black salvation" in 2000 asserted that "The pan-Africanist dimension of reggae music and its specific intellectual and emotional appeal are largely explicable in the light of the African origins of its Jamaican pioneers. Their historical experiences and social struggles are reflected in the works of several of their musicians who see their musical profession partly as the acceptance of a challenge to fulfill a duty". Reggae musicians and Jamaican members of the African Diaspora drew inspiration from Africans leaders like Kwame Nkrumah, Sekou Toure and Jomo Kenyatta. These leaders identified with the struggles of the Jamaican people.

In Jamaica itself, Ska and other early reggae artists used their songs to express their determination for change. Bob Marley (the most prominent champion of the black liberation via the world of reggae) expressed the desire to fight in his timeless song "Get up Stand up", which focuses on the need to not be fooled by popular beliefs but to become alert and fight for your right. He then encapsulates the slavery and freedom link with the song *Redemption Song*. In this song Marley laments the suffering on the slave ships and the regeneration of strength in the slaves such as the Maroons in Jamaica who refused to be subjugated. Marley does this by saying "my hand was made strong by the hand of the almighty". He then brings the listener to the present, exhorting leaders and the people whom he refers to as those "Forward in this generation", to strive for the final triumph. However, he acknowledges the formidable challenges and laments the elimination of black leaders such as Martin Luther King Jr. and Malcolm "X" and asks "How long shall they kill our prophets, while we stand aside and look?" He ends by asking the new generation to remember that it is just part of the structures of oppression but they need to hold firm against all types of might and continue to sing the songs of freedom. Asante-Darko sees redemption song as part of the militant songs of freedom, patriotism and Messianism. He describes the essence of the song as follows

"Redemption Song", by Bob Marley, for instance, begins with the narrator's account of a personal experience in which the persona is a victim of pirates who kidnapped and imprisoned him in a "bottomless pit". It is followed by his enslavement, continues with his eventual fortification by God and ends with his redemption and triumphant living. This story acquires universal significance in two stages: first, as the speaker turns to address the audience to identify with his past misery and present triumph. Its rhetorical merit resides largely in the appeal to the audience in the rhetorical question: "Won't you hail to sing redemption songs?". The second is when the speaker, convinced that the proof of his argument is self-evident, establishes a close bond between himself and the audience by appealing directly to them to "emancipate yourselves from mental slavery". He deepens the solidarity he seeks by introducing the second person plural of the reflexive pronoun in the sentence "None but ourselves can free our minds." The subsequent appeal for courage and commitment is given in the reassuring way that neither "atomic energy" - the symbolic expression of the military might and technology of the oppressor - can halt the advance of freedom. Then comes the strategy of infesting the audience with a sense of guilt with the aim of having their acquiescence and active adherence to the cause he advocates. This is also stated in a rhetorical question: "How long shall they kill our prophets while we stand aside and look?". The speaker concludes with a logical refutation of any potentially deterministic objection to his opinion. By all these he implies that active dedication to the said cause, rather than pristine apathetic nonchalance to his admonition, is the right way to fulfill "the Book" of Prophecy.

Following in the tradition of what Asante-Darko calls militant songs of freedom, is Bob Marley's song *War*. In this song, Bob Marley, using the content of Emperor Haile Selassie's speech justifies confrontation with the oppressors. The attendant action to the racial superiority thesis is summarised in the following words: "Until the philosophy which holds one race superior than another, is permanently discredited and abandoned; everywhere is war" (there will be war). These words denote the moral bankruptcy that underpins this philosophy, for such a stance will only generate conflict and destruction. Bob Marley equally makes specific mention of the need to rid Africa of colonialism in his song *Zimbabwe*. In other songs, he preaches the idea that the black people will overcome the barriers imposed by the oppressors. Such a determination to succeed drives Bob Marley in his song *Rebel* to label colonialism and oppression as the Babylon System; a Vampire. He emphasizes that determination to resist stating "We refuse to be, what you wanted us to be; We are what we are: That's the way it's going to be. If you don't know!" And then asks people to rebel.

Peter Tosh's *Equal Rights* speaks to the yearning for recognition, which is associated with dignity. Together they support the reconstruction of the Blackman's identity and restoration of self-worth. Peter Tosh's songs such as *Equal rights* and *I am the Toughest*, speak to the need for advocacy for equality and social justice. He reminds the listener of the fact that talking about equality and justice is not enough. It must be practicalised in the lives of people. In his song *African* he reminds the listener of the oneness or common identity of people of African descent on the mother continent and in the Diaspora, by saying " Don't you mind your nationality once you are Blackman, you are an African. In his song *I am the Toughest*, Peter Tosh tries to assert the notion that the Blackman is tough and can do exceptionally well in anything, better than those who seem to think that he cannot. The song is an admonition to black people about their qualities and capacity to do things for themselves.

Other reggae singers such as Burning Spear, Culture and Black Uhuru, proclaimed freedom in many songs. African reggae singers such as Alpha Blondy used their songs to praise historic figures and also to voice opposition to African struggles such as Apartheid with his song *America, break the neck of Apartheid*. This internationalization of reggae music in the late 1960s and the 1970s enhanced the struggle for political independence in countries such as Zimbabwe, Namibia and Mozambique, which were still under colonial rule. It also provided rich words of inspiration to young people, including messages of positive self-image and striving to achieve life goals.

Jimmy Cliff in Tamale,   Bob Marley   Jimmy Cliff
(Front row, far right)
Ghana, 1989

Hip Hop artists such as Afrika Bambaataa, DJ Kool Herc, and Grandmaster Flash mirrored Pan-African direction of Marley and other reggae musicians. Ulysses Ronquillo observes that Afrika Bambaataa played both the literal and figurative role of a warrior. Bambaataa was a member of the Black Panther inspired People's Organization for War and Energetic Revolutionaries, or P.O.W.E.R. However, he gave up his militant vision following the death of his cousin. Like Malcolm X and Marley his initial war rhetoric inspired by people like Elijah Muhammad and Louis Farrakhan, soon gave way to advocacy for peace, love and economic emancipation. One of the emerging themes from the civil rights movement was the realisation that political emancipation did not end all suffering and that Black Nationalism needed to achieve other goals in the realm of economic and social progress. Malcolm X, Martin Luther King Jr. and others realised the need for reconciliation with the oppressor groups and redirect energy toward improvement in other domains of life. To them, confrontation sapped excess energy required for improving the wellbeing of the black population. Such a message of reconciliation and moving forward was later epitomized in the actions of Nelson Mandela in South Africa. Mandela's philosophy of reconciliation with White South Africa demonstrated the incalculable relevance of not seeking the path of war when there is opportunity to pursue peace and improve the wellbeing of the oppressed. In my view, black identity and vision across the world began to shift towards this goal in the post-Apartheid era.

The reality of black identity in the 21 century

The efforts of independence leaders, civil rights leaders, musicians and other advocates of freedom and equality, bore fruits. Many black populations are independent of the bondage of political structures that subjugated them under colonialism and intentional marginalisation . Even apartheid has been abolished in South Africa and a rainbow nation, in which all people are free to dream of individual pursuits irrespective of colour, has become a reality.

However, by the end of the 1960s and early 1970s while the civil rights movement was still fighting for improvements in the lives of African Americans in the USA, and reggae artists were becoming louder with chants of Afrocentrism, the momentum of hope was already beginning to disappear in Africa itself. The leaders in many African states were beginning to fail in the quest for improved wellbeing. Instead, they had begun the creation of kingdoms of hell; a subject I discuss in chapter 5.

In the Americas, the existing social and economic inequalities have not been completely eliminated and more work is required to achieve equality. However, economic inequality has not become a strong rallying point unlike political inequality, which had previously galvanized everyone to take collective action. In other words oppressive pressure of social and economic inequality has not pushed people enough to forge a common identity and action. Thus the pendulum of inequality still swings against African Americans in education and employment, and race prejudice remains.

To this reality, Isom (2007) wrote about the experiences of African Americans as follows: "Living in a predominantly White Anglo-Saxon society conveys a message – at all times – of being a minority, whose voice is drowned by the dominant cultural voice of the majority. This has served to perpetuate the inability of African Americans to take control of the definition of their own identity and muted the full achievement of objectives of the civil rights movement. A similar situation exists in most African countries which are beset with massive currents of internal oppression, "self-mutilation and destruction", beginning with issues of citizenship recognition and depleting /confused societal values.

PART II
VALUE CRISIS IN POST-INDEPENDENCE AFRICA

Chapter 5
Religion and the Crisis in African Values

One of the biggest problems facing Africa today is diminishing values around the individual's relationship with community and society. That is, people are losing values around the notion of obligation and service to local community and the nation state; and what as a collective we need to aspire to achieve other than money.

Values in Africa are a complex mix of traditional African, Islamic, colonial and western church values. This has generated a crisis in which many African people have abandoned positive traditional African values. At the same time, we whole-heartedly embrace the negative western values, and either refused to practice or corrupted the positive Western, Church and Islamic values. It is important to note that the ideology of African and Black Nationalism is built around the value of pride in black identity. However, it does not prescribe anything else of substance beyond identity. And it has become obvious that mere pride in the self does not teach us how we ought to build peaceful and prosperous societies, which will allow our sense of pride to endure to the point that others will recognise and respect that African identity.

Under colonialism, the European colonialists depicted African societies as people who had no values. In one such example, the French colonialists expressed fears that the evil and diseased Africans will pollute their "superior values". Frantz Fanon was infuriated by the French colonialists' depiction of African values in such a demeaning manner. And at the threshold of African independence Fanon wrote:

*"..As if to show the totalitarian character of colonial exploitation the settler paints the native as a sort of quintessence of evil. * Native society is not simply described as a society lacking in values. The native is declared insensible to ethics; he represents not only the absence of values, but also the negation of values. He is, let us dare to admit, the enemy of values, and in this sense he is the absolute evil. He is the corrosive element, destroying all that comes near him; he is the deforming element, disfiguring all that has to do with beauty or morality..."(p.40)*

A particular depiction of this lack of values in Africans by a Monsieur Meyer stated in the French National Assembly incensed

Fanon. Monsieur Meyer stated in the French National Assembly that:

The Republic must not be prostituted by allowing the colonised people to become part of it. All values, in fact, are irrevocably poisoned and diseased as soon as they are allowed in contact with the colonized race". The customs of the colonized people, their traditions, their myths -- above all, their myths--are the very sign of that poverty of spirit and of their constitutional depravity (p40-41).

These words of the coloniser, which Fanon found offensive, are in my view, more or less prophetic words that have come to symbolise the African malaise. To a large extent all positive values from our African traditional cultures and even Christianity and Islam, which we gullibly embraced, have been poisoned and diseased. Fanon had argued that the derogatory comments by Monsieur Meyer should lead to only one action against western values and that is:

" .... we must put the DDT which destroys parasites, the bearers of disease, on the same level as the Christian religion which wages war on embryonic heresies and instincts, and on evil as yet unborn........The Church in the colonies is the white people's Church, the foreigner's Church. She does not call the native to God's ways but to the ways of the white man, of the master, of the oppressor. And as we know, in this matter many are called but few chosen" (p.41) .

Unfortunately Fanon's recommendations about what to do with the Church did not take place. Rather, the exact opposite occurred and in my view for better and for worse. Fanon had hoped that after colonialism, Africans would spit on the Whiteman's values because of the manner in which native values were characterised as evil and inferior He articulated this hope in the following words:

During the period of decolonization, the natives' reason is appealed to. He is offered definite values, he is told frequently that decolonization need not mean regression, and that he must put his trust in qualities, which are well tried, solid, and highly esteemed. ....The violence with which the supremacy of white values is affirmed and the aggressiveness which has permeated the victory of these values over the ways of life and of thought of the native mean that, in revenge, the native laughs in mockery when Western values are mentioned in front of him. In the colonial context the settler only ends his work of breaking in the native when the latter admits loudly and intelligibly the supremacy of the white man's values. In the period of decolonization, the colonized masses mock at these very values, insult them, and vomit them up.

If Fanon was alive today, he would be hugely disappointed. Africans unreservedly embraced these colonial church values, which Fanon detested and perceived as the root cause of the Blackman's oppression. Africa's embrace of the church is total and disastrous, not simply because Africans profess the Christian faith but because its negative aspects such as domination and exclusion have been championed and its positive aspects have been corrupted to the extent that the European Priests who preached the religion a century ago would not recognise the church in Africa. By wholeheartedly embracing these values, we also embraced the principle of Affirmative Subjugation (which I discuss later) and created our "Kingdoms of hell with a million prayers".

Creating "Kingdoms of Hell with a Million Prayers"

Independent Africa was a collection of new states built on colonial political structures, imbued with values of the colonial church promising a new Kingdom of Heaven. However, the reality on the ground was a poisoned political and economic situation evolving hand in hand with changing values; the emergence of kingdoms of Hell. The affirmative subjugation deriving from extreme gullibility in relation to the knowledge and values of the colonialists transformed Africans into loyal soldiers, championing the oppression of their own kind in the name of foreign faiths - Christianity and Islam. In these "kingdoms of hell", began the hollow practice of foreign religions characterised by millions of unceasing prayers. Surprisingly these praying populations had become part of a system which was depleting the values essential for maintaining social solidarity, wellbeing, and enhancing economic development.

Africa is a very religions continent and prayer is an integral part of every facet of life, as well as everyday activities. However, the "heaven" and blessings promised by various religious beliefs (Christianity, Islam and Traditional African Religions) have not changed the lives of the people for the better. Political leaders have systematically and unashamedly created, through greed and corruption, a sea of poverty, disease, hunger, hatred and lack of compassion. In these "Kingdoms of Hell", Africans yell out millions of prayers, hoping for deliverance from this "hell". I am of the view that the failure of religious practice is an important part of the creation of Africa's kingdoms of hell.

The concept of religion hinges on the supernatural and the mental construct of belief (in God or something) is one of the most invaluable psychological tools of all humankind, because it helps to conquer our fears and instill hope in our very existence. That is why religion has had the extraordinary capacity to be employed as a medium for both positive and negative events in human history, including inciting wars, hatred, racism, slavery, and paradoxically, love, compassion, peace and development. Religion is thus a neutral force like power or authority, and can be used positively or negatively to direct the destiny of human societies.

It is not uncommon to hear many Africans attribute our under-development to colonialism. However, as much as this long-ago experience could have contributed to our predicament, the contemporary situation in Africa has more to do with ourselves- our values and aspirations. As the developed world gallops away with scientific, technological and material progress and peace, the struggle for survival provides more fuel for the poorer communities in Africa to reach out to the supernatural for help through their prayers. One could argue that it is only in Africa that the prediction of Sigmund Freud that there will be a decline in religion with scientific advancement is yet to unfold.

Faith in the supernatural and in the teachings of various religions, local and foreign, is profoundly strong in Africa. Some have described the over-reliance on religion to the detriment of more scientific explanations of things, as one of the most formidable barriers to Africa's progress. I argue that to a large extent, it is not belief in itself that is the problem, but the selective attention to only some aspects of the teachings of religious thought and corrupting those teachings. Africans see religion as nothing more than prayer and this extreme essentialisation of prayer precludes other forms of thinking around how religion could support their own wellbeing. Religions teach more than worship. They teach values, which can be the most invaluable assets of a community. However, most Africans' attraction to and acceptance of Christianity and Islam emanated from a strong identification with mystical aspects of Jesus Christ's life and miracles or the power of the words of the Quran to miraculously transform their lives. It was not driven by the values of the religions. I shall return to this later.

In 2005, up to four articles appeared on Ghana Internet news sites, eulogising the role of religion and religiosity in African development. These articles were suggesting that believers could support Africa to develop through a strong faith in God and the work of good Christians. In my opinion, these articles were equally suggesting – implicitly – that the glories of Europe were created through prayer. I argued then that the European "Kingdoms of Heaven" were created not through prayer, but instead through the values that we seem to completely disregard as part of religious practice. I opined that Africans' appreciation of what Europeans have is more about the overt (that is the great cities, architecture, good living conditions / live style) than it is about the underlying values (mental, attitudinal and convictions about life/community) that make European societies "Kingdoms of Heaven without prayer". While Europeans cherish the philosophy that "The true meaning of life is to plant trees under whose shade you do not expect to sit (Nelson Henderson), many Africans only want to plant trees under whose shade they must sit. Some Africans are prepared to destroy such trees if they know they have no opportunity to enjoy the shade. In short, there is a discrepancy in values and this huge discrepancy between the values taught by religion and the practices that inform daily lives, provides justification for religious analysts to conclude, without reservation, that religion is truly the opium of the masses in Africa.

The practice of religion in Africa is dominated by three faiths - Traditional African Religion, Christianity and Islam. And irrespective of the creed, religious practice revolves around two dimensions, which I choose to label as "The Spiritual" (giving birth to rituals) and "The Conscience" (giving birth to humane laws and actions). Most contemporary European countries have taken away the spirit and rituals of Christianity, but kept its conscience and humane laws/actions, creating what I call "Kingdoms of Heaven without prayer" for their people. The contexts of these "Kingdoms of Heaven" allowed for the creation of systems that uphold the values of truth, honesty, kindness, and hard work, in addition to food, shelter and peace. The populations of Europe therefore have all the necessities of life as it is envisaged would be obtained in Heaven/paradise, even with little or no prayer. Africans on the other hand, have kept only the spirit and rituals of Christianity and Islam, and abandoned the conscience and humane laws of these faiths. Through an extreme essentialisation of prayer and miracles, to the exclusion of all other requirements, African nations have created on the contrary, "Kingdoms of Hell with a million prayers" for their people. The contexts of these "Kingdoms of Hell with a million prayers" are breeding grounds for lies, dishonesty, corruption, hate, wickedness, and all manner of injustice, in addition to hunger, disease and misery. This is one unique paradox of religiosity, which appears to defy explanation, but which certainly can be explained as emanating from historical, psychological and methodological developments of religious practice.

The Conscience of Religion and the Crisis of African Values

Many Africans think of religion in a one-dimensional way – it is only about prayer and miracles, and so they can pray for days and seek miracles without doing any other work. However, many will be surprised to realise that in the teachings of the Traditional African Religions, Christianity and Islam, more is required of believers in relation to the welfare of the members of our society (including justice, kindness, honesty and compassion) than prayer and miracles.

African peoples and leaders perhaps pray more than many other nations on earth, but they have not internalised the conscience of religious thought that sincerely recognises that all people (of different ethnic/language groups) are equal as sons of God (Bible), and creation of God (Quran), and that every single citizen needs the basic necessities of life. For this reason, there is a growing and demonstrable absence of compassion in ordinary people and African leaders in all countries. The lack of values around honesty has grown into deep-seated dishonesty, which translates into deceit, lies and the general corruption ravaging the continent. Indeed, the tendency to lie is so pervasive that one is tempted to think that in meeting with African people in many social contexts perhaps only the exchange of greetings can be taken to be true. All other exchanges will be riddled with lies. This is also true with very overtly religious people, who frequently tell lies, even in their prayers. Yet according to the religious books, it is only in a society of truthfulness, kindness, and compassion that prayer becomes truly meaningful, and this is perhaps why the prayers of Africans are of no good. Unfortunately, many prominent religious leaders only flash their credentials as the best minds, with the fear of God and who should be listened to, yet remain silent on corrupt practices and other incredible atrocities of governments. They are associated with corruption in high places. Given this situation, there is pessimism in regard to employing reform in religious thought as a way of enhancing good governance and promoting development in Africa.

Religions teach great values such as hard work, responsibility, tolerance, respect and compassion for others. These are not just noble ideas or ideals, but constitute the embodiment of the aspirations of societies, and what makes societies peaceful and progressive. The protestant ethic was used as a foundation for the values of hard work that led to the development of broad pursuit of scientific knowledge, improved food security and compassionate societies of Europe. Yet in Africa, the extreme religiosity focuses more on prayer, miracles and almost nothing else. Do Africans, as professed Christians, Muslims and/ practitioners of traditional religion, hold and cultivate the spectrum of values to mirror the extreme adherence to prayer? Do religious adherents think about the values that are missing in their lives?

In my view religious practitioners ignore important values. When Jesus Christ (in the New Testament) overturned the tables of the moneychangers in the Temple in Jerusalem, it was because the misplaced values and actions of those men were undermining the purpose of God's Temple. Africa is desperate for answers from God, but it may be that God has over-turned the tables of Africans because they undermine the true purpose of God's Temple- the Heart, which dictates those honest words of prayer that issue from our lips. In Africa's case, the words of prayer are dishonest and selfish.

There is no doubt in my mind that, with all our trooping to churches, mosques and shrines, true morality is rapidly dying in the larger African society and it manifests clearly in our politics and politicians. Morality and social conscience are replaced by diseased-hearts of dishonesty, greed, hate, and lack of compassion, which fuel unreserved desires to be rich at the expense of the happiness of our communities. It is so common to hear some African Christians and Muslims say that they will not help someone because he or she is not a believer in their faith. What is wrong with us, as people whose forefathers, for generations, were neither Christians nor Muslims but mostly traditional African believers? Compassion is the child of the heart (like faith), and until there is a compassionate change in our hearts, we are in for the long haul, because God, (according to Quran Chapter 8:53) will not change the condition of a people until they change what is in their hearts.

What is astonishing is that ordinary praying Africans are ready to defend the misdeeds of governments and politicians, even when they are in conflict with the principles of their religious convictions, and even with the knowledge that their corruption has resulted in a lack of drinking water or health services in their own communities. We need to make conscious judgments about our actions and those of our politicians and how these actions impact on everyone. It is equally important for each one of us to remember that our own actions contribute to this misery, and our prayers alone will not alter our situation. Until we do this, our practice of religion, indeed our faith and prayer, will qualify to be defined (in the words of Ambrose Bierce) as a request to God that the laws of the universe be annulled on behalf of petitioners (Africans) who are confessedly unworthy of God's Mercy.

The key question here is: How can we create the European style "Kingdoms of Heaven" rather than the existing "kingdoms of hell" backed by our millions of prayers? We have failed to use religion to guide the development of our values towards total community salvation, wellbeing and development. Our understanding of religion is all confused and what we want from God in our million prayers is either completely incomprehensible or selfish. What is clear though, is that many Africans want God to give all of the good things required in their communities to them as individuals for their personal material salvation, and whatever happens to all others is unimportant. And because we have lost sight of this problem, we tend to believe that our suffering is the result of not praying enough, when in fact it is that we failed to use our intellect. As one grows to appreciate the extent to which European nations have cultivated the values of kindness, honesty and love without comparable expression of religiosity via millions of prayers, you begin to feel that the current expression of faith and religiosity in Africa is nothing but a huge furnace melting away all of the pockets of kindness in our hearts. In fact, the more religious we become the more we lose compassion for our communities. Social solidarity, which emerges from compassion for others, is the backbone of a society's social capital. Though all societies possess social solidarity, the quality and intensity of the solidarity diminishes with changing values. In Africa, solidarity has been diminishing since the coming of foreign religions and their gradual and total influence on our thinking. Ministers and "Prophets" in the name of Jesus and God are fast emerging as corporate entities, building empires and huge real estate by manipulating poor Africans who desire special prayers. We see huge buildings proclaiming to be the houses of God but the House of God is not a building but the hearts of the worshipers. These 'men of God' are dancing tango with corrupt public office holders who are able to pay hundreds of dollars to these modern-day prophets who have no shame. Poor African people pay huge amounts of money for special prayers offered by heartless 'men of God', who are the exact opposite of Christ's legacy. When will these poor believers realise that if money was needed for special prayers, then Jesus Christ would have asked payment from those who were cured, healed and brought back to life? How on earth can we Africans ask for God's mercy when we have no mercy for others? The mercy of God encompasses all things, but that mercy will be hard to give to people who have no mercy for other men.

Karl Marx called religion the opium of the masses. Sigmund Freud on the other hand called it human infantile neurosis and Bierce called it an explanation of the nature of the unknown. Sadly, we may find that these definitions appear to perfectly describe the practice of religion among Africans today, because we don't seem to know what faith and religion truly mean. There is misapplication of faith and prayer among all African Christians, traditional worshippers and Muslims. We believe in God without knowing what exactly God wants us to do when society's leaders are not doing the right things. Our blind faith in religion leads to silence, with only one utterance ' God will help and deliver us', instead of standing up to our leaders, requiring the best from them, and changing our own input into how our societies function.. Can there be an excuse before God for one who pockets the money meant for the construction of a water facility or health facility for an entire community? Bob Marley's words echo more powerfully') here ' Is there a place for the hopeless sinner who has hurt all mankind just to save his own soul?' Yet there is silence everywhere, even in the churches, mosques, shrines, and in the hearts of the praying politicians who are taking exclusive part in the eating of 'the cake that belongs to all'.

Religion has anesthetized the population into the 'silent suffering Africans' who have simply accepted the gloomy situation as our fate, and erroneously concluded that it is our destiny. What we fail to realize is that our destiny is alterable by employing the power of intellect and hearts, which God and nature gracefully bestowed upon every human being (at no cost). Africans appear to have chosen not to use their intellect and hearts constructively and our situation is therefore a self-imposed destiny. Sadly, as Ambrose Bierce noted, destiny is 'A tyrant's authority for crime and a fool's excuse for failure'. Thus, Africans have only taken religion as an excuse for failing to take responsibility, to rise up to the tyranny of leaders and their collective failure. Therein lies the genesis of Europe's

Kingdoms of Heaven without Prayer and Africa's Kingdoms of Hell with a Million prayers.

Chapter 6
Africa's Value Crisis: The Role of Christianity and Islam

Africa is facing a values crisis, which is characterised by confusion about what is right for our societies and what individuals should aspire for and demonstrate in their inter-dealings with others for the greater good. This situation has external and internal, historical and progressive traits and each of these is worth considering in this chapter. The stark reality is that Africans have lost the values that sustained our communities in the past, and which are indispensable to our future as nations of people who believe in the ultimate power of God to deliver us from suffering. I contend that contemporary African values have both the fingerprints of the history and teachings of foreign religions- Christianity and Islam and an internal evolutionary character post colonialisation.

Reverend Harvey Sindima, the great Malawian philosopher and writer commenting on the subject of values, associated the current value crisis with liberal philosophy in Africa, colonialism, the teachings of the church and the western school. He lamented the fact that African traditional values continue to be eroded. Echoing Reverend Sindima's view, I contend that our values of community collective good (have changed to values of individual good through association with foreign religions. Indeed, the historical, psychological and methodological developments of foreign religious practice in Africa have contributed to the change.

Traditional African Religions versus Christianity and Islam

African Traditional Religion has a communal focus. It teaches that the individual is connected to the community from birth to death and beyond. That is to say that the connection to the community is forever. Individual actions bring both individual and collective reward/punishment to his family and community. In fact, the individual reward and punishment are tied to the community reward. As practitioners of African Traditional Religion, Africans were all part of the community; inseparable and worked for the good of the community. In this sense the individual had to strive to be good for the collective happiness of the community. This was a necessary

58

requisite in order that the individual could be endorsed as one of the good ancestors on his/her death. Thus, the individual's continuous connection to the community was unavoidable, even after death. This teaching ensured that every member aspired to the goal of having a good rather than bad or unpleasant connection with his/her ancestral community in death. Such a strong integration of faith, actions, rewards and punishments enhanced community collective wellbeing.

On the other hand, Christianity and Islam teach that good deeds bring good rewards to the individual, and in the judgment to come, the individual will live in heaven/paradise with his/her family. This conception of the reward for religiosity is a complete departure from traditional African religious teaching. In Christianity and Islam the individual earns his/her a place in paradise, where he/she has no connection to his original community. Thus, to do anything against one's own community does not require answering to the entire community in death; for punishment in relation to sin is directed at the individual. This teaching did not and does not have the exact communal component found in African Traditional Religion. This is perhaps the genesis of the change in our values in relation to our communities. Islam and Christianity thus, brought far-reaching changes in our beliefs and values and the way we perceive our actions in relation to our communities. The importance of this change can be observed in the fact that some Africans, in spite of strong faith in Christianity or Islam still have lingering fear of their traditional gods. And if they have lied, or have been dishonest, are more likely to choose to swear by the Bible or Quran rather than their traditional god. The reason for such a choice is that the retribution of the Christian or Islamic God will take place on some faraway day called the "Day of Reckoning", while the retribution of the traditional African god is believed to be immediate and on the entire family.

Even though both the Christian and Islamic faiths have influenced African values, Christianity has had a broader effect across contemporary Africa because of its association with colonialism. In my opinion, the changes (positive and negative) in our values of kindness, compassion, and hard-work, have got to do with two important developments:

1.   The collective effect of the historical development of Christian teachings, the psychological orientation induced by

the context of colonial rule in which Christianity was taught, and the methodology of the church.

2.   Our own selectivity of the teachings and practices of the church.

Historically, Christianity existed in Africa even before it got to Europe, and the Orthodox Christianity of North and North–East Africa was inherently different from the Christianity that came from Europe, which dominates today's Africa. The contemporary African brand of Christianity, which I choose to call *Christianity of Colonisation* was tainted with the ideology of domination, and separatism, and came on the bandwagon of the colonialists who set up the context in which it grew. As a consequence, it is not surprising for many African Christians to think that they are different from, and better than, non-Christians, and therefore do not want to associate with their family members who believe in Traditional African Religion. The colonial mentality of separation and exclusion informs this attitude.

The domination and separation ideology of the colonialists nurtured values that lacked the humility and solidarity of the church. Consistently, the relationship with Africans was defined in master-servant terms, rather than in terms of two equal servants of God. It is worth noting that at the dawn of African colonisation, the ideology of domination was re-emerging from the end of absolute Catholicism in Europe into the egalitarian era of Protestantism. Domination as an ideology was on its deathbed in Europe but found new lease of life in colonial Africa. Christian missionaries, in spite of their humility, dictated and inspired by the word of God, operated in the context of the new political atmosphere of colonialism; with a philosophy to dominate. This partly explains why the early European missionaries in Africa failed to condemn slavery in the first 300 years. Indeed Christian theology provided basis for the missionaries' broad and unfounded assumptions that African societies had few or no values worthy of emulation or recognition and had to be fed values issuing from Christian principles.

Although the missionaries made honest attempts to teach all of the core Christian principles of honesty, humility, compassion and service to community among others, these teachings could not be divorced from the context and ideology of colonialism. The methodology and teachings of the church became tied to the colonial administration's agenda, and it is evident that the first African Christians were members of the church as well as agents of the colonial system. These African Christians were exposed to two competing streams of values- one stream of humility in service of God, and the other stream of prestige, power and domination and exclusiveness as part of the colonial establishment. Between these two competing sets of values, the colonial value of domination was more attractive to the psychology of the African. Thus, the first African Christians were more products of the colonialists than they were of the true church. These colonialists-tainted values of exclusiveness and acquiring power to dominate have subsequently been passed on to our current generation of civil servants and politicians.

Today the attempt to dominate followers of other religions is prevalent and creates disharmony in our societies. In some aspects our political and religious leaders are keen on domination and exclusion, to the extent that believers of traditional African faiths and Islam are ostracized or oppressed. In one peculiar situation in Ghana, students of such faiths are forced to attend Christian worship in public and private schools by powerful school principals who profess the Christian faith. This has been a clear case of domination ideology visited on young innocent people for decades without reprieve from government until the 2012 election in Ghana. During the 2012 election campaign, the President John Dramani Mahama admonished school chaplains and headmasters not to force Muslim students (and for that matter other believers) to attend Christian worship because it was against the constitutional provision stipulating freedom of religious expression. This statement drew hostile reactions from some Christians. They did not only argue the fact that students of other faiths must attend church services in privately established Christian schools, but also in publicly funded Christian-dominated schools. Some stated bluntly "If you go to Rome, do what the Romans do".

I found it profoundly astonishing that a practice such as forcing non-Christians to worship in a church, which belittles Christian worship, still finds support among some Christians. I wrote an article reminding Ghanaians that this uninformed support for such practices was perhaps issuing from a colonial mentality inherited by the African church. This mentality borders on ignorance about the purpose of worship and disrespects Christian worship. Firstly, forcing non-Christian students to worship in church violates their human rights and imposes psychological torture on the young people. Secondly, it is completely at variance with true Christian principles, and Jesus Christ would never accept that this be visited on any human being. How then can some Christians get it so wrong? Thirdly, are the school principals really saying that God would love to see a young boy or girl sitting in his House of Worship upset, angry and yet singing words of praise with contempt?

Here we see that those Christians supporting this practice have not really cultivated the pure Christian value of respect for others' choices and freedoms. It is important then, that schools observe one of the most fundamental and irrefutable principles of worship and religious expression; the principle that worship comes from the heart. Undoubtedly, forcing non-Christian students to worship does not pass this test. It is simply, psychological violence and no deity of any prescription or description (be it from the perspective of Hinduism, Judaism, Christianity, Buddhism or Islam) would be happy to have a person worshipping with strong reservation or abhorrence. Jesus Christ, as a unique embodiment of humility and tolerance would not appreciate such practice. In other words, in no religion will God be impressed with a young person worshipping in a state of trauma, reservation and half-heartedness.

These kinds of issues exist in different forms in other countries, suggesting that colonial Christianity is still with us and those who endorse coercion in religious practice are either emulating the colonial church, which used intimidation in mission schools to convert African children, or repeating the common mistake of organised religion. The common problem with organised religion is that it often loses its moral focus and instead directs its attention to power and control. It therefore becomes political, inhumane, insignificant and detached from the real issues of human kind. And history has taught that political religion, whether in Judaism, Christianity, Islam, Hinduism or Buddhism has always brought more misery than peace to humankind.

Selectivity of Values in the Teachings of Religion

In a conscious process of selective exposure, most African Christians are consistently choosing to imbibe the values cherished by the domination ideology of the colonialists, rather than those of humble service to God and the community. In terms of values, both Christians and Muslims have replaced hard work, giving and worship with something else and all these lead to a crisis in our values. I now turn attention to a discussion of the selectivity of values in relation to hard work versus prayer and miracles,

62

displacement of worship with vanity, entertainment and egocentrism, and the issue of receiving versus giving.

Values of Hard work versus Prayer and Miracles.

While European and American Christians, in line with the values underpinning the protestant ethic, perceive hard work and prayer as central to religious expression, Africans prefer only prayer and miracles. Most Africans accepted Christianity and Islam for mystical and economic reasons and not for the particular values they espouse. The Miracles of Jesus Christ were very attractive to the superstitious and magical-minded Africans who often perceive every earthly event as emanating from the spirits. Thus for most Africans, as people who believe in the power of the mystical to save, the most attractive thing is not Christ's moral teachings but rather his mystical nature and actions. So there is the concentration on prayer and enacting miracles to cure, to get rich and to succeed. This is also true of early African Muslims who practiced mystical Islam and therefore preferred religious orders such as the Tijaniyya, among others, which harnessed the miracles of the Islamic faith.

The attraction to miracles explains why in the last two decades, traditional churches in Africa such as Catholic, Anglican, and Methodist are losing membership to the more Evangelical and Pentecostal churches, who spend every minute "delivering miracles, cures and protection from Satan". African Christians have corrupted the purpose of Christian worship. They are obsessed with fighting evil spirits and almost nothing else, and since only the firebrand preachers of the Evangelicals and Pentecostal churches can deliver us from such evil spirits, using Christ's miracles, many will continue to flock there. Go to most church services and you will notice that very few are talking about values such as hard work, compassion and community improvement. The same applies to Muslim communities. Many West African Muslims are also pre-occupied with the use of Quranic verses and mysticism and so in countries stretching from Senegal, Mali, Burkina Faso and Guinea to the coastal nations like, Sierra Leone, Ghana and Nigeria and Togo, Mallams or Alfas, concentrate on these mystical practices and have little interest in espousing values about other aspects of daily life and interdealings.

The focus of religious leaders - priests, pastors, and prophets, on miracles and the redemption from evil spirits is quite surprising because a very important principle and value of the Reformation was the cultivation of the protestant work ethic. Martin Luther and John

Calvin's work on the nature of freewill led to the notion of the call to vocation. According to John Carroll in his work *The wreck of western culture*(2004), one of Calvin's main ideas, that differed from those of Luther, was the notion that "a calling" by God as obtains in the Christian teaching was not limited to a spiritual sphere alone. ' Luther had stressed the importance of the religious sense of God's Calling but it was Calvin who started the protestant transformation of everyday activity in the world into the central form of religious devotion. Carroll writes that it is through Calvinism that work becomes holy. The protestant form of prayer becomes the individual at work, head-bowed, concentrating, hour after hour, day after day, year after year producing something that is of quality, done to the best of their abilities. Calvin believed that a vocation was means to learning God's will and a discipline that helps tame the passion and reduce restlessness. The protestant work ethic was transformational and took hold in the west. Calvin touched the dispositional core of the western society, who perhaps for the first time realised that work was part of service to God. The effect of the Calvinist protestant philosophy on the entire western society was profound. It transformed the protestant faith and work ethic and also western society. In America, the protestant work ethic led to industrial development and huge leaps forward in relation to productivity, adherence to family life and service to society. The church in Africa has preached these principles and it is also clear that such an approach to religiosity was already a part of African Islamic thought for more than 1000 years. The prophet of Islam had said in several Hadiths (collections of Mohammed's sayings) that those who worked to feed their family and society were more deserving of God's grace than those who prayed every day. Given that the notion of hard work as devotion to God is a central teaching of Christianity and Islam, it is rather surprising that so many African Christians and Muslims are among the laziest, preferring to pray to God and expecting God to give them all they ask for in their prayer and doing less hard work. Herein lies the fact that Africans have refused to take up or live up to the true dictates of their foreign faiths. This is related also to the corruption of worship.

Corruption, Misplacement And Vanity Of Worship

Related to the issue of prayer are the issues of corruption, misplacement and vanity of worship, as an important part of the religious conundrum in Africa.

Firstly, the spread of Islam in Africa from about the 7th century onward had different effects in West Africa to that of the rest of Africa. Whereas Islam in North, East and Southern Africa maintained its orthodoxy, in West Africa its spread also coincided with the corruption of its focus. Muslim preachers were also traders who wanted to awe the non-believers by emphasising the power of the words of the Quran to deliver miraculous outcomes from the healing of diseases to winning wars. The latter supported the conversion of the kings of West African empires including Mali, Songhai, Gonja, Hausa Mossi, Mamprusi and Dagomba. Kings in these empires were believed to be successful by employing amulets and other insignia grounded in Quranic verses. In later centuries, the Kings of Ashanti will rely on Muslims from the older empires such as Mossi, Dagomba, Mamprusi, and Gonja to support their war and expansionist effort. From these historical developments, Islamic practice among Muslims in West Africa became focused upon miracles and what I see as mechanical adherence to the five daily prayers, with limited regard for the problems of the wider society. Today, many Muslims focus on the miracles of Islam and zealous adherence to prayer in a mechanical rather contemplative way. Practitioners' demonstrate few values which promote collective wellbeing. Muslim leaders are known to support social vices and corruption and more importantly, have done little to curb the growing intolerance of other belief systems as preached by Al-Qaeda. Recently Al-Qaeda type Islamic movements, such as Boko Haram whose ideology promotes hatred and inhumane actions, are spreading across Mali, Niger and Nigeria. The stance taken by these people is contrary to the tolerant Islam that characterised the days of the glorious Mali and Songhai Empires, and which made Timbuktu a centre of learning and commerce form about 1300 AD.

The issue at stake is that the intolerance people express surprise some of us who grew up in large families where different members of the same family practise all three major faiths -African Traditional religion, Christianity and Islam. A Nigerian friend recently related a sad story about his uncle, a Muslim and his childhood friend, a Christian which illustrated the reality of recent changes in tolerance to religious difference brought about by Al-Qaeda and fundamental Christian propaganda. As children these two friends and their families used to celebrate Christmas and Muslim Eid festivals together. Both families would present food and gifts and enjoy the days together. Now in their late 50s, the friends lamented how Nigeria has changed in the last 10 years and soured the relationship between the two families. All of a sudden, Imams and Pastors are saying that Christians and Muslims should not befriend people of the other faith. What a tragedy! My friend blamed it on Al-Qaeda and the many commercially oriented so called "Born Again" Christian churches and I tend to agree because this has never been the stance of traditional churches such as the Catholic and Anglican Church in Ghana, where I grew up. As a Ghanaian who grew up with people of different faiths in my family, community and schools, I had a complete indifference to people's religious background. They were just children like me and I didn't really think of my friends in terms of their religion. I therefore find it difficult to fathom why people preach exclusion and intolerance.

For African Christianity, the core beliefs, values and focus of church teachings, such a belief in God, working hard and praying for salvation after death, are replaced by African metaphysics. The African Christian wants to go to church to pray for three key things: First; deliverance from his/her evil aunt or uncle who is a witch/wizard bent on killing him/her family and children. Second; how to counter the power of witchcraft with the divine power of Jesus Christ. And third; using Christ's miracles for anointed healing. This type of Christian teaching will be alien to the White priests who brought the colonial church to Africa. And if they wake up from their graves and see/hear what the church is teaching, they will be completely confused. I often wonder what Fanon would think of the church if he were alive and whether he would have preferred the Whiteman's church to the corrupted one of our times because of its more damaging effect on our society today.

To have a sense of the pervasiveness of this corruption, one has to understand that the linking of the church to such mystical African beliefs have served to undermine objective thinking in many more ways than the orthodox Christianity based on simple worship of God to achieve life after death. European Christians did not hold such beliefs and taught that God was more powerful than the Witches and magicians. For this reason, early African Christians started to discount the role of witchcraft and strong superstitions and although this did not completely eradicate such beliefs, Christians did not harp on such superstitions. For this reason, I believe that Fanon's lamentations about African values and the church have taken a turn for the worse. I also believe that Fanon was certainly right in that the Church was like a poison to Africa. However, in today's Africa, the preacher is not white but black, and is inflicting the most unkind wound of all on the natives.

Lamenting the problems of Christian worship in America, W. Robert Godfrey, Edward Vasicek and Monte Wilson wrote coherently about the misplacement of worship in some Churches. Their views are so vital to any analysis of the African situation that I find it necessary to quote extensively from them. In an article titled *How a Worship Format is Destroying the Evangelical Church* written in 2011, Edward Vasicek mourning how worship has been displaced in evangelical churches with music and emotional feelings said that:

During my lifetime, many evangelical churches in American have moved from Bible-oriented gatherings to music-dominated meetings. Many evangelicals previously viewed music as a "warm up for the sermon." But the paradigm has changed in many churches. The most important change is what the word "worship" is now used by clergy and laity alike to refer to the religious feelings aroused by music". Biblical sermons have given way to self-help lectures or emotionally charged sermons with lots of illustrations—replacing the previous Psalm 1 mentality.

He observes that the problem is not contemporary music, seeking to have meaningful worship through songs of praise, etc. The problem is simply what he calls displacement. When we displace the knowledge of the Word and solid doctrine with music (whether we call music worship or not), we are no longer under the lordship of Christ. The Christian life includes public worship, but the highest form of worship is hearing and doing the Word of God.

To me, this concern about the benefits of good worship translates better to the idea that worshiping God and being a good Christian is about the values you take out of the Bible and the church, which guide your dealings with others and the society. In Africa, the paradigm shift is from the word of God to music and miracles to deliver people from evil spirits. The Africanisation of the church is in full swing. All we want from Christ and his church is "deliver us from evil spirits and bad thoughts of our evil family members and neighbours". No one is preaching about what values we need to take to our homes, schools, offices, and to run our national institutions. There is nothing but Vanity in Worship and the most favoured are those who speak in 'tongues' and purport to be immersed in the Spirit. The miracles are so frequent that you wonder how the "prophets" of today manage to perform them when even the great Biblical personalities like Abraham, Moses, Isaiah, Jeremiah and others only did so occasionally. Well, never mind, the important thing to note is that these modern prophets exert a malevolent influence over the minds of the millions who flock to their churches regularly to seek 'prophetic anointing' and 'protection from spiritual enemies'.

The corruption of the belief system to focus on delivery from evil witches and superstitions has increased the appeal of Christianity to the indigenes of Africa, but it has also plunged Christians into thinking more about miracles and deliverance. And this is something that the clever "prophets" of today's evangelical, corporate-type churches in Africa have capitalised upon. It is a strong 'persuasive marketing which fools poor people into donating their homes, cars, monies, blocks of land and other property in order to receive miracles and deliverance from special men of God. This type of church is spreading across Africa and being championed by "Prophets" from Nigeria, Ghana, Kenya and others. Recently the Nigerian "prophets" of this new African church have descended on Botswana, and established more than 20 separate churches promising all things. Everyone has been swept off their feet by this type of African-touch evangelism, which can heal spiritual ailments caused by witches in your family as well as physical illnesses including HIV/Aids. The media has reported of wealthy Batswana rendered poor by their gullibility and an uninhibited desire to donate their wealth. How can a Nigerian prophet heal you when there are so many of your kind in Nigeria who are yet to be healed?

Music, Worship and "Pavarotti Pastors"

The use of Music was supposed to be for praise and worship not for entertainment. However from the 1990s, the use of gospel music in worship was embraced both for entertainment and worship. As gospel musicians became rich from their activities, many artists began to produce music that meshed with hip-hop and became multi-million dollar corporations. They reasoned that if the pastors could make money from tithes and offerings, nothing stopped them from making money by turning worship into entertainment. The pastors then began moving into bigger buildings to accommodate more worshipers from diverse backgrounds. In these merger churches they geared their worship activities towards more sophisticated entertainment and became entertainers rather than pastors.

Dr Monte Wilson wrote about the use of entertainment in church worship as well as its attendant vanity in an *article Narcissism Goes to Church: Encountering Evangelical Worship.* His well-articulated presentation is quoted here to paint a picture of situation as a prelude to discussing its impact on Africa.

He relates a scenario of what happens in modern evangelical worship services lately, trying to answer the question of whether or not "Evangelical Worship" is an oxymoron.

He takes the reader through one such worship session describing the preacher as Mr. Rapport who starts his service by asking everyone to stand and greet one another and walks up and down the aisle shaking hands with the members, kissing babies and, in essence, acting as if he were running for office. The purpose of this act is likened to the evidence of the modern proof of God's presence: Warmth and Fuzziness. For the preacher "The service must have the correct ambiance. People must feel wanted, even needed--or they will go elsewhere". This is a very telling change in what worship is about, and Monte Wilson observes the normal service used to begin with Bible reading and prayer, declaring the congregation's allegiance and submission to Christ. Today, our allegiance is to "user-friendliness" and therefore some churches will open with a cheery choir special or a hap-hap-happy song sung by the musicians. The purpose of this act according to Monte Wilson is to convey the message that

After all, happiness must mark the service. We are a happy people. We have something to offer you. We are exciting and positive--and you too can be like us if you join our church!" Compare this with the ancient liturgies that began with, "O God the Father of heaven, have mercy on us miserable sinners." Whoa! That won't do. What a downer. This certainly won't work in a church that wishes to make everyone feel good about himself.

Monte Wilson describes the music leader as a combination of Pavarotti (albeit without the training), Dick Clark and Liberace who cajoles, exhorts and waves his arms. He explains the depth of meaning in the lyrics of each song, he cheerleads, he cries--all on cue. What matters is that everyone has a great, happy, ego-renewing experience. He notes that the most important thing today is the preferences and tastes of the people and not the scripture and so people want songs that excite, move and gratify without over-taxing the mind or soul.

The most interesting part of Monte Wilson's article is the preaching itself. He observes that the preachers begin with a story not necessarily intended to carry the message of scripture but one that must assure everyone that the preacher:

"...is glad they are there; he is capable of wowing them; he is a real master of the pulpit; and just plain folk, like all of them. If he fails to accomplish one of these objectives, he is in trouble. If he fails in two, his job is in jeopardy.... the real need is psychology and entertainment. The man must move the audience. He must make them feel loved, needed, wanted, appreciated, cared for ....Content is secondary, if it is relevant at all. What matters is that the minister is personable and able to make every individual present feel like he is talking just to him".

In much of Africa and especially in West Africa, examples of this type of modern day Pastors and "Prophets" yearning for the spotlight and the accolades of the congregation abound. The most prominent include Pastors and "Prophets", such as T.B. Joshua, Mensah Otabil, Duncan Williams and Eugene Asare. According to Monte Wilson they yearn to go on an ego trip for both the worshipper and themselves. They move, cry and woo people because they just love being on centre stage to cultivate reverence and admiration from men, women and children who all will stand in awe of their skills. In this calculated performance the awe of the preacher's brilliance is always sought because he is only successful if people fall on the altar and say that they have been saved by his special skills and divine touch.

Monte Wilson says that however, when there is no response from the people - No one is saved; No one spoke to him of his brilliant performance, No one fell down at the altar, then he is a failure. No one appreciates him. No one knows his toil, his anguish--his insecurity and the ravenous hunger of his ego for approbation". This is a case of egocentrism mixed with delusion because even in the presence of Jesus Christ people did not always expect a miracle and certainly Christ was not seeking to awe people but to give them a message for their own lives. Monte Wilson thinks that this is certainly a joke of worship and asks,

Where do Christians go who do not want a circus but the sacraments? Where does a hungry seeker go to be fed with doctrine deeper than messages that can be boiled down to, "Don't worry, be happy"? Where are the Houses of Prayer? I was taught that, "You get what you fish for." We fished for people who wanted to be entertained. Now, if we pull the plug on the spotlights, they will go elsewhere.

In Africa today, churches still preaching something else other than entertainment or redemption from evil spirits to the African Christian, are no longer getting the attention. No wonder the traditional churches are losing their flock. Summarising, Monte

70

Wilson says: "Is it any wonder that the average Christian is led around by his experiences and feelings rather than by God? The modern church--the place where he was to encounter God and learn of his ways--has told the Christian through symbols, teachings and structures that his needs and feelings are paramount!" It is also telling Africans that what happens in societies and after death is not as important as deliverance of evil spirits. This is certainly in my view, a shift in Christian values and the big question is: What are Christian leaders doing about the values we need to make our nations into the Kingdoms of Heaven that we have been praying for? In the same vein, how are African Muslim leaders endeavouring to preach against the social vices, the evil visions of Al-Qaeda and the hatred of others faiths? Muslim leaders should preach the tolerance of Islamic teachings that nurtured the harmonious environments of Muslim Spain that endured for 700 years in which peoples of all faiths- Christians, Jews and Muslims prospered.

Values of Receiving versus Giving

The positive values around giving and helping others from Christian and Islamic teachings, which were in sync with our traditions have been negatively acquired and transformed into a central part of our thinking and everyday actions. For this reason, most Africans prefer to receive than to give and today, we witness an evolution of these negatively acquired values at the individual and collective levels. They significantly affect our thoughts, tastes, desires, actions and preferred ways of doing things. We are left with distorted values and excessive concentration on how to receive, even against the dictates of the scriptures and our traditional African religious philosophies. As individuals and as nations, we prefer to receive from others than to give. This is in spite of the teachings of the scriptures that 'Blessed is the hand that giveth than the one that taketh' or 'It is more blessed to give than to receive.' (Acts 20:35,Holy Bible,) or 'The upper hand is better than the lower hand' (Islamic teaching from Hadith). In fact, the desire to receive rather than give has grown to become (shamefully) an acceptable and cherished value for our societies and nations, making us into the most prominent beggar nations on earth. When those religious books and traditions teach the value of giving, it is not only something God likes but it is also something that is appreciated in the secular realm. However, just look around our families and entire nations and you realise that we are attuned to asking for more help and hardly ever think of becoming self-sufficient. Whereas many non-African countries are reluctant to ask for help even in extraordinary times, our African countries have no shame at all in seeking help even in ordinary times. Take the case of Japan in the 2011 Tsunami trying to go it alone. That speaks volumes about self-respect and pride. And yet many African nations are asking for foreign aid even during ordinary times, with no sense of what we could do over the long term in order that we only ask for aid during extraordinary times. It appears as though many of us are now tempted to think that we cannot survive without receiving help from somewhere else.

This is a big crisis of values and we are aware that those who beg have no power to influence anything. Beggars simply generate disrespect for their persons and offer themselves on a platter for insult, pity and ridicule. Is it any surprise we are looked upon with pity, disrespect and scorn? What is worrying is that our huge natural resources are either left untapped or under tapped. If we held the value of giving in high regard, we would seek ways by which we could exploit our resources to their maximum potential and to position ourselves to give to others. We would then be fulfilling the religious principles and promise of giving to others. However, at this stage, we are so inflexible in our minds about praying for and receiving help from God that we cannot switch to thinking about what we can offer to others in our societies and overseas.

Conclusions: The African condition has roots in adopting values of religiosity and a view of the world that embraces mysticism. African nations are the most religious in the world and yet they have only managed to create kingdoms of hell with millions of prayers. It is important that religious leaders preach a different set of values, such as hard work that is accompanied by prayer; honesty that allows us to remain cognizant that our communities suffer gravely when we act dishonestly within a system that is not capable of detecting or bringing us to justice; de-emphasis the notion that prayer is supposed to fight evil machinations created by enemies within our families and community, 'instead emphasise prayer to receive wisdom to create resources for our community. Only in this way can we give to others, rather than waiting to receive all the time. Finally, when politicians and ordinary people who profess strong religious beliefs imbibe the wrong values and become exclusionary in their approach, we usher in a future of doom and gloom for Africa; a perpetuation of our Kingdoms of Hell, with a million prayers.

Chapter 7
Crisis of African Values: Affirmative Subjugation and Progressive Community Values

Affirmative Subjugation in Africa

Values are the social fibre of a society. They play an indispensable role in transforming societies and should be cultivated and preserved with care. If a society loses focus on creating, upholding and preserving its cherished values, then it is certain to decay. I have argued that the African value crisis has roots in subordinating positive African values to foreign ones. I have coined this term Affirmative Subjugation as the exact opposite of Robert Fox's idea of Affirmative Orientalism. Fox's idea of Affirmative Orientalism aligns perfectly with Edward Said's Theory of Orientalism, which laments the asymmetry between the power of the West and the East. In Orientalism, Said, describes the Oriental other as passive, voiceless people who do not possess any capability to represent themselves.

In Affirmative Subjugation, the Blackman is passive and indifferent about what is originally his own. He subjugates his thought, beliefs, values and languages to that of western thought, beliefs, values and languages. The population is extremely gullible and accepts western ideas and beliefs almost without second thought. This is much in line with Edward De Bono's phenomenon of 'intelligence trap' and its opposite "the blindness of ignorance", where people swallow every idea hook line and sinker. They don't make any serious analysis of ideas, which are presented to them because they feel that it comes from a superior thinker. This is the root of Africa's "Affirmative subjugation"

Africans have submitted themselves to the dominance of Western values including an extreme adherence to Christianity in a rather unhelpful way. African intellectuals reject their own traditional cultures and irrevocably endorse western cultural values and knowledge in a way that can be described as Affirmative Subjugation. The subjugation is so pervasive in many instances that it constitutes an uninhibited gullibility, which results in a tendency not to accept anything African if there is a western alternative.

73

The problem of Affirmative subjugation becomes manifest in the tragic failure of post-independence governments to entrench the principle of indigenization when it came to choosing national languages. In fact there is a manifest and systematic attempt by Governments to prioritise these languages to the neglect of indigenous ones. Indeed when independent African countries use foreign languages as national languages and when free individuals in our societies on the mother continent choose not to teach our own native languages to the new generations, then we have a serious problem. This has led to the grim reality that we indirectly reinforce the learning of foreign languages and now there is widespread use of European languages, as the medium of communication in African homes. These examples of unforced subjugations have contributed to the rapid decline in the use of African languages by African people who have no European ancestry. They have also led many Africans, without pride, to think that mimicking Englishness or French-ness is the greatest thing that could ever happen to an African.

In 2010, I wrote a piece on this subject as it applies to Ghana and suggested that Ghanaians, and for that matter all Africans, who are not teaching their native languages to their children may be doing so intentionally or unintentionally. Although we could accuse those who do so intentionally as being ashamed of their native languages, there is also the role of power in language learning such that the pressure of a more dominant language results in minority groups abandoning the use of their languages. It is common knowledge that a key factor determining the capacity of one language to dominate others is power, in its different manifestations. The contemporary economic power of the west derives from political and cultural power; and this was also the case for the great empires of old. The empires of old were able to expand the dominance of their languages by the use of political power to create other forms of power such as coercion and social sanctioning to compel others. Astonishingly, this is not the case within African countries, at least not in the last 50 years. And yet it is common today that African children will be born and raised among their own tribesmen in Africa and be unable to speak their local languages. This is usually so because parents prefer to speak the language of the colonial masters. Such a thing is unthinkable in Asia. It is obvious that the need to learn English for example, is due to international pressure, but does not derive from the power of coercion or social sanctioning, managed by the colonial master, Britain. The power of English derives from the pressures exerted by majority language groups who often, slowly but inevitably, exert power by persuasion, habituation or inducement on smaller groups. In the exercise of these types of power by dominant languages, minority groups will use the dominant languages because it is more convenient to use them (persuasive power of the dominant languages); they get so used to using the dominant languages to the extent that they automatically use them without giving it a second thought (power of habituation); and finally they get rewarded and applauded for their use of the dominant languages by members of the majority group (inducement). Africans living in Europe and America today find it hard to get their children to speak their mother tongues properly because the children find it convenient to speak English (persuasion); the children become used to using English in and out of school (habituation) and they are able to achieve academically and socially at the same level as all other children (inducement). Nonetheless, if we were conscious of our tendency to subjugate, then we would make some effort to preserve some of the important legacies of our forefathers. The question that needs to be asked is how come Asian language speakers always get their children to speak their native languages?

Names, Ceremonies and Affirmative Subjugation

When I was living in Norway in the late 1990s, I had a very interesting discussion about African names. Five African friends and I met in the heart of winter for lunch, in the warm environs of a quiet restaurant in Oslo. We discussed several issues and then came to the meaning of our names. Two of us had our names rooted in native African languages. While one person had a Christian and African name and the other two had all their names deriving from Christianity/Europe or Islamic/Arabic traditions. One of those with a name deriving from the non-African sources insisted that all others were not religious enough, while the rest of us believed that he was not African enough. The argument was quite intense but betrayed the reality that in Africa today traditional names with loaded meanings are vanishing in place of more popular/universally recognisable names such as John, Margaret, Edward, David, Mary etc. It is not uncommon to see an African with no affiliation to Europe or America (through earlier migration) called Phillip Mitchell. Sometimes it looks strange and embarrassing. However, this form of Affirmative subjugation is another step towards the loss of African traditional values. In African societies names are more than just their actual meanings. They denote a connection with ancestry, a link between the past and the present and a signpost of the era and/or context of a particular child's existence. All these are being forgotten and will vanish with time. In Ghana, naming children according to the days of the week continues in most families especially among the Akan. However, the practice is disappearing in many other areas. Many West African Muslims, including those in Hausaland and Dagomba have been using Arabic names like Mohammed and Ahmed to the extent some families cannot remember when any of their grandfathers had a traditional African name. Fortunately the trend seems to be on the retreat in the last decade with many children being given traditional names in addition to names associated with their religious affiliation.

Affirmative Subjugation permeates all domains of life from religious beliefs to marriage and social events/practices, as well as to the goals and content of education. And although taking on ideas and practices from other cultures is a necessary feature of cultural dynamism, Africa's uninhibited gullibility is a disaster. The danger of a seemingly uninhibited gullibility is that you don't question and critically evaluate the new ideas and therefore you are more likely to misinform yourself and misapply the values. The other troubling issue about the African situation is that we are more likely to accept values in the domains of the meta-physical and ostentation and not those relating to scientific knowledge and attitude to work. As observed earlier in this book, Africans' acceptance (and understanding of Christianity is limited to faith, prayer and miracles, and focuses less on the more pragmatic aspects of life from these teachings. This coupled with beliefs in superstition has, in my view, served to undermine African thinking and has set in motion an almost irreversible negative impact on Africa's development.

Individual versus Community-Good Values

The institution and cultivation of good or positive values that inform and direct actions are indispensable to the happiness of our communities. African traditional cultures are generally collectivist rather than individualistic and therefore values and actions lean towards communality. Thus African cultures and traditions had emphasised honour, ancestors, family and community as embedded in the philosophy of Ubuntu and others. The reality today however, is that our values around community-good or wellbeing are giving way to values focusing on individual-good. In an evolving post-colonial system the question that needs to be answered by African nations, is whether we prefer an 'I' culture or a 'We' culture, that fosters collective wellbeing. For centuries, collective community solidarity and wellbeing have been at the heart of African culture but as the value of collectiveness gives way to individuality, it is important to still remind ourselves that community-oriented values will also enhance individual wellbeing.

Many African nations and communities seem to have lost, or are losing, values that motivate individuals to want to give to others and take pride in giving to others and the community. The tendency to want to receive from others means that we do not generate enough creative solutions for the benefit of Africa and the rest of the world. Many African people ask why we are unable to harness our local resources to meet our own needs. The answer might be that we want others to think for us, like the manner we expect to fall from heaven when we pray for God's help. If this is the case, then we are expecting foreign people to come and tell us what to do with our natural resources to generate broader benefit.. Why do we wait for someone (outsider) to tell us what we need to do to generate better community health, prosperity and wellbeing? To some readers of this book I am perhaps just harping on something insignificant, but can you imagine that some communities will never clean their filthy drains or gutters until a sanitary inspector orders that they be cleaned? Such directives from a sanitary inspector usually draw "fire" and anger from the people in the community who feel disrespected and yet they complain of mosquitoes and sick children. We need to recapture communal thinking and pragmatic solutions, which often go beyond individuality. Without focusing on this value of collective wellbeing we are failing to think deeply about how to harness our natural resources and are continuing to wait for someone else to think for us. It is this passive attitude or apathy which makes us aspire to serve no other person but ourselves. Unfortunately we even do that badly; hence the greed and under performance of our leaders.

Honesty is an important value for community wellbeing, yet we hold a distorted view of when the value of honesty should apply to ourselves as individuals and when it should apply to our neighbours, our community and national institutions. We want people to be honest when they deal with us but it is ok to be dishonest when we deal with others, including our governments and our national institutions. For example in Ghana, politicians and civil servants justify pilfering funds and resources from government institutions by making the assumption that the government is not an entity that feels the effects of pilfering. In fact, they forget that whenever the government loses a dollar, someone may miss out on access to medicine in a hospital, or someone does not get paid to provide food for his family or someone somewhere gets no water to drink. Elsewhere, I have written that no nation can develop Africa but us. Through thinking and placing value on sustaining what we have, we will realise that foreign aid (in the forms of food, money etc) is not development. And that we are losing sight of the fact that aid from Europe or America, in all forms is merely the end-product of the creative process, which reflects the values our friendly donor nations have cultivated for themselves. How much money do we need to borrow before we are able to provide water and basic health for each community at a sustainable level in our countries? No amount of loans will suffice until we cultivate the value that it is everyone's responsibility to maintain and sustain what we have in our communities, otherwise we have to borrow these monies a hundred times over and achieve nothing. In fact, a systems approach to looking at our communities would lead to a systems-value-conceptualization i.e. conceptualizing our values in terms of what we need as communities and as peoples (Africans). We need to revert to values that uphold the survival and efficiency of our entire systems - in this case, our villages and communities. In such an exercise, we cannot dismiss the role of honesty, responsibility and pride in using our intellect and strength to create and give to others. We have to win the battle between values of individual good and values of community or collective-good.

Values of Functionality versus Values of Ostentation: Flattering the Dead

Today, we in Africa have cultivated a new value system, which I call flattering the dead and punishing the living. The modesty required of zealous religious practitioners such as we have in Africa would dictate that we also aspire to hold values and tastes that are modest and which serve specific positive functions for individuals and society. This implies that ostentation is to be avoided. However, our choice of clothing, birth and funeral rites and development priorities reflect ostentation rather than functionality. Our society lavishes on big funerals compared to Europe and America, with specially designed coffins costing thousands of dollars although our children have no food, clothing and educational materials. Families borrow money to show that they too can provide a lavish funeral and after the event they sink into depression. In a country of poor people such as Ghana, with no efficient water and health delivery system, the population spends over one billion dollars each year on expensive coffins and accessories. This practice can be likened to withdrawing one billion dollars from the Bank and burying the money in our cemeteries, and then asking God to help us feed and clothe our children, or asking the European union to give us a grant to build a school. We certainly think that it is better to punish the living in order to flatter the dead.

Our governments prioritise and support projects of ostentations including flashy residential buildings, Cathedrals and airports. These leaders do these things so that when they die they will become immortalised in those ostentatious monuments. However, the paradox is that while such ostentatious monuments often have first class roads leading to them, there are no functional roads to the nearest hospitals. Examples of such ostentation is the building of the largest Cathedral by former Ivory Coast President Houphet Boigny costing millions of dollars in a nation that has poor access roads, beyond the ones going to big cities, and an inadequate health care system. In Zaire, Angola, Nigeria, and the Central African Republic of Congo such ostentatious projects have caused their populations to continue to live in unimaginable poverty. If this crisis of values is not recognised by our African elite and leaders, there is little hope that we shall ever come out of the doldrums.

CHAPTER 8
Nationalism, Ethnicity and The Oppressor Within

The Promise and Failure of African Nationalism

The dream of many African leaders during political independence was to create progressive societies in which nationalistic feelings and effort would nurture an agenda of Pan-Africanism, egalitarianism and improved wellbeing. On the African continent, the Pan-Africanism ideology was not only expected to infuse a sense of black unity but also to free the African people of economic dependence on the colonialists. It was therefore not surprising that the euphoria of hope and prosperity that came with political independence was effusive and African leaders dared to dream of a harmonious and prosperous Africa.

The first president of Ghana, Kwame Nkrumah wrote the following about this dream of egalitarianism in his work entitled "African Socialism Revisited" (1967):

"We know that the traditional African society was founded on principles of egalitarianism. In its actual workings, however, it had various shortcomings. Its humanist impulse, nevertheless, is something that continues to urge us towards our all-African socialist reconstruction. We postulate each man to be an end in himself, not merely a means; and we accept the necessity of guaranteeing each man equal opportunities for his development. The implications of this for socio-political practice have to be worked out scientifically, and the necessary social and economic policies pursued with resolution. Any meaningful humanism must begin from egalitarianism and must lead to objectively chosen policies for safeguarding and sustaining egalitarianism."

Many other independent African leaders preached similar messages and most Africans believed that successive national leaders will pursue the positive agenda of black emancipation inspired by the Pan-African movement with vigour and resolute vision. Undoubtedly, post-colonial African leaders in countries like Ghana, Zambia, Guinea, Senegal, Kenya and Nigeria were emotionally charged with the idea of African political and economic emancipation. They aimed for comprehensive development of all sectors of the new nations to mirror the standards in Europe and America.

The first crop of post-colonial African leaders was a mixed bag of true nationalists in total pursuit of the "Dream of African Glory", and those in pursuit of personal empire building, driven by the desire to become the "New "Raj" replacing the "Colonial Raj". For independence leaders such as Kwame Nkrumah of Ghana, Julius Nyerere of Tanzania, Kenneth Kaunda of Zambia and Sekou Toure of Guinea, their determination to achieve meaningful development for their nations was unquestionable. However, the dictatorial and empire building tendencies of some leaders such as Jean-Bedel Bokasa of Central African Republic, Abeid Karume of Zanzibar, and for some people, Kamuzu Banda of Malawi, were glaringly visible within the first two years of assuming power. And it is leaders like Bokasa, Karume and Banda, who became role models for the coming of the true dictators, who were, in my opinion, the architects of Africa's Kingdoms of Hell. Thus, beginning in the late 1960s, the broad hopes and dreams of better times in most African countries had begun to evaporate with dictators usurping power.

The Emergence of the Dictators

In thinking about what Africa's development could have become, one can say that perhaps the biggest tragedy is the fact that in some countries many of the first leaders were kicked out of office early on and replaced by empire-building dictators. First, the arrest and killing of Patrice Lumumba, the first legally elected prime minister of Belgian Congo, on 17 January, 1961, under the watchful eyes of Belgian soldiers began the creation of one of Africa's biggest kingdoms of hell. According to Georges Nzongola-Ntalaja, (Professor of African and Afro-American studies at the University of North Carolina and author of *The Congo from Leopold to Kabila*), Lumumba's assassination is rightly viewed as Congo's original sin. He writes that the assassination, which took place less than seven months after independence (on 30 June, 1960), was a stumbling block to the ideals of national unity, economic independence and pan-African solidarity that Lumumba had championed. It was a shattering blow to the hopes of millions of Congolese for freedom and material prosperity. Lumumba, he observes, was interested in the unity of the country and the welfare of the people in contrast to other rivals of the time such as the CNL leadership, which included

Christophe Gbenye and Laurent-Désiré Kabila, who were more interested in power and its attendant privileges.

The greatest legacy that Lumumba left for the Congo is the ideal of national unity and his execution saw the arrival of one of the most corrupt and brutal dictators in the person of Mobutu Sese Seko. During his more than 30 years rule of the Republic of Zaire, Mobutu presided over political and economic vandalism. He plundered the country's resources, saving billions of dollars in European accounts and generated intense ethnic divisions, which still rage, 50 years on. Although Zaire was rich is a range of natural resources, the living conditions of the population were far worse than many less endowed African countries. Indeed both Mobutu and Laurent Kabila, who became president after 30 years, did little to improve the welfare of the people. Kabila's son is still ruling and there is no peace or progress in sight for the Congolese people.

Silvanus Olympio of Togo was assassinated in 1963, paving the way for Nicolas Grunitzky to become president. General Nyasingbe Eyadema who helped Grunitzky to power, overthrew him in another coup in 1967. He then began a long stable period of dictatorial rule with no ambition for developing the country or the citizens' capacity to move their country forward. The story in Togo, for reasons of its peace and stability, departs from the many stories that followed the coups in countries such as Nigeria, Zaire, Uganda and Angola. In each of these countries, the coup leaders were corrupt and brutal, plunging their countries into economic collapse and tribal conflict.

In Nigeria, the overthrow of Tafawa Balewa's government witnessed the accentuation of ethnic divisions, culminating in the Biafra civil war that reduced much of the country to rubble and rolled back the clock of economic development. Increased levels of poverty fueled more ethnic divisions and corruption, slowly making Nigeria into one of the most corrupt nations in Africa. The election of Shehu Shagari in 1979 coincided with the height of Nigeria's prosperity deriving from her status as the 6th largest producer of oil in the world. Unfortunately, it also marked the beginning of the obsession with acquiring political power. The overthrow of the Shagari Government in 1983 marked the return to Military rule that was brutal and facilitated the entrenchment of corruption and open embezzlement of state funds by military elite. At the height of the embezzlement, President Saani Abacha, the architect of many coups was found to have deposited billions of dollars in foreign banks and large amounts of cash were found in his home. Although the return of Obasanjo to power as a civilian president was perceived as an opportunity for change and development, the corruption culture in politics was further accentuated, not only at the Federal level, but also most seriously at the state and local government levels where Governors rarely account for their stewardship. In fact, ordinary Nigerians lament the level of corruption across all levels or strata of the society and feel that, it is impossible to reverse the situation. To people who have lost any hope for Nigeria, this level of non-accountability means that the country is heading for the abyss. In a country endowed with huge resources, up to 60% of the more than 100 million people, live under shocking levels of poverty, without basic health and social services, epitomising in all its grandeur, Africa's "Kingdoms of Hell with a Million Prayers".

In Ghana, the coup leaders of 1966 accused Nkrumah of being a dictator, but they realised after seizing power that they had no clear vision about development of the Nation. In the three years of military rule that followed, they were only interested in increasing the salaries of the military. In their idleness, they allowed many state owned small and large-scale manufacturing industries to go to waste, setting in motion Ghana's economic decline. Half a century later, many Ghanaians acknowledge the difference between a dictator with national vision and those in other countries who were personal empire builders. In spite of the many mistakes of Nkrumah, it is abundantly clear that he did not amass personal wealth and for this reason many Ghanaians applaud him and he stands apart from most early African rulers.

Emperor Bokasa of the Central African Republic and Iddi Amin of Uganda are two dictators accused of cannibalism and yet the two leaders were different in how they contributed to the creation of Africa's kingdoms of hell. Although Iddi Amin was brutal and anti-Asian, recent analysis of his legacy shows that he was less corrupt for the simple reason that he did not amass personal wealth. Bokasa was perhaps the most wasteful and brutal leader, championing the killing of his rivals, marrying women from different countries in very lavish ceremonies and wasting his country's meagre economic resources.

In all these countries, while the economies were declining, the dictators were swimming in luxury seemingly oblivious of the problems besetting their countries. They also began to harness the power of ethnicity to maintain power.

Tribalism Kills Nationalism in Post-Independence Africa

I have always imagined what life in Africa would be like if the vision of nationalism and egalitarianism was underpinning governance in all countries. The correlation between the institution of good governance and societal values that promote egalitarianism and democracy on the one hand, and improved wellbeing on the other, is fairly obvious. And one can conclude that the failure of African governments to institute these conditions, explain in part, the continent's turmoil and unceasing conflict. The lack of egalitarianism began with the creation of nation-states in Africa \when the colonialists also manipulated existing ethnic relations. In almost all African countries there is unambiguous evidence of the tacit complicity of the colonisers in the creation and perpetuation of what is now clearly a minority marginalisation discourse and social structure. In Rwanda and Burundi, colonial oppression and machinations created a toxic relational atmosphere between Hutus and Tutsis. In West Africa colonialists sought to subjugate smaller ethnic groups under larger ones in moves that both distorted the existing histories and changed the symmetry of power.

Ethnic tensions were rife in Africa prior to colonialism. However, it is clear that colonial arrangements accentuated the sharp divisions and bitterness existing in many countries and western colonial powers need to openly interrogate their own complicity in that toxic mess.

At independence, ethnic groups across African countries lived with the inheritance of the colonial experience, which allowed dominant tribes to perpetuate material and epistemic violence on minority tribes. In order to reverse this negativity many African leaders were keen to institute nationalistic feelings, using nationalist slogans and educative processes, but the outcomes were very different in different countries. The idea of pursing broad nationalistic feeling and a development agenda was accepted by the populations of many countries. However, some leaders soon deviated from these paths, allowing tribalism to take hold. Thus, within the first ten years of independence, tribalism had killed nationalism in most countries.

The examples of Tanzania, Ghana, and Uganda illustrate these different outcomes. Perhaps Tanzania is the most successful African nation to solidify nationalistic feelings through President Julius Nyerere's Ujamaa project. Nyerere is said to have emphasised repeatedly that ethnicity was not to be used as a criterion for providing access to public services and resources. And today ethnic tensions are quite subdued in Tanzania, which has allowed inter-ethnic marriages to become the norm; a great example for the rest of Africa. In Ghana, President Kwame Nkrumah guided by the national motto "Freedom and Justice" pursued an inclusive development policy, which witnessed the building of schools, health facilities, road infrastructure and factories across the length and breadth of the entire country. However, the agenda of nationalism went terribly wrong in Uganda. President Milton Obote's initial vision of building a unified Uganda based on his "Common Man's Charter", soon gave way to persecution of tribes such as the Baganda. It came to a head when he sent the army to shell the palace of the Baganda King Kabaka Mutesa II, which led him to seek asylum in England in 1966. From then on ordinary people began to call Obote's slogan "Common Man's Shut up". Milton Obote began a systematic process of favouring people from his own ethnic and regional area over others and thus became a champion of the process of "tribalism killing nationalism". Today Yoweri Mosenveni continues to strain ethnic relations. He is widely accused of favouring his own relatively small Banyakole ethnic group against the much larger Buganda and others such as the Acholi of northern Uganda. Museveni is said to be promoting ethnic tension as a way of maintaining power. Andrew Mwenda in a column in 2010 observed that Museveni continues to project an image of a democratic leader who is keen to establish grassroots democracy but in reality he is straining ethnic relations and creating new avenues for official corruption.

Malawi's President Kamuzu Banda tried to develop Malawian nationalistic values based on African traditions. His philosophy was derived from the matrilineal system of the Chewa and tribes of Malawi that share the matrilineal system common to some African groups. However, the practice was criticised as entrenching the hegemony of the matrilineal Chewa. The Patrilineal tribes such as the Ngoni, Tumbuka, Nyanja and Nyakyusa felt marginalised and therefore President Banda's claim of creating national unity and solidarity only sharpened ethnic resentment. His inability to create more unifying values across the nation lay in his failure to identify a common value system such as Ubuntu that permeates all of Malawi's ethnic groups. Leroy Vail and Landeg White in the work on women's role in Malawian nationalism, observed that as culture broker for the Chewa, Banda had a broader vision, however, in formulating an ideological statement for his ethnic group alone, he has instead equated 'Malawian-ness' with Chewa-ness. In short, Banda emphasized uniquely Chewa cultural attributes, instead of secular Malawian 'nationalism'. Thus Banda killed nationalism with tribalism.

In Nigeria, the jostling of the three major ethnic groups from the North, South East and South West, led to the death of nationalism in a most profound way. Nigeria witnessed one of the bloodiest civil wars (The Biafara War) in post-independence Africa. The wounds of that war are yet to completely heal. Even after nearly 50 years, both victors and losers continue to lament this sad event, not only because of the suffering and inhumanity that it engendered, but because it killed true nationalism. In Zaire, the euphoria surrounding the coming to power of Patrice Lumumba died after his capture and assassination in 1961. Mobutu saw his power as dependent on protection from the Belgians and the people of his ethnic group. From such a position he immediately alienated other ethnic groups and the divisions, which eliminated national consensus, have remained to this day.

Since the 1960s such conflicts across Africa have claimed millions of lives in direct fighting but also through ethnic marginalisation, which slowly claims the lives of millions of people over decades. People living outside of Africa are perhaps only aware of the case of Rwanda, and Burundi where such ethnic tensions have been so brutal beyond belief. However such tensions deriving from the creation of modern states abound in almost all African countries because the European colonialists ceded power to different ethnic groups above others. These conflicts have made it difficult for many Africans to hold patriotic attitudes towards their nation states. In other words, nationalism is subordinated to ethnicity.

Ethnic Relations and "Black racism"

Ethnic hatred and exclusion are clearly "black racism", which has contributed to the absence of coherent and consensual thinking when it comes to national development in most African countries. Scientists and Psychologists have noted that the use of the human cognitive faculties is better in situations of positive emotions than negative ones, especially anger. In Africa, anger and hatred towards rival ethnic groups does not allow for objective thinking around national development because policy makers are always thinking about how to marginalise rival ethnic groups rather than what will bring the best economic advantage to total national development. Today ethic domination has coupled with the inequalities created under colonialism to cement a strong foundation for continuing marginalisation and epistemic violence against minorities in relation to their opportunities for social and economic development. And it is very common to read derogatory comments from people belonging to dominant tribes against minority tribes whenever the latter raise their voices demanding equal opportunity.

There is widespread hatred between ethnic groups and in some countries the level of intolerance between some ethnic groups is so high that one wonders whether any value system, religious or otherwise could teach such deep-seated hatred. Sadly, the interpretation of both Christianity and Islam in Africa has culminated in a dominating discourse of exclusion. And the politicians are the first to feed this discourse and also commit resources to nurturing the gulf between ethnic groups. These issues are mild in some countries and very entrenched in others.

In Nigeria, the intense ethnic divisions have also unfortunately become intertwined with religious divisions. It is impossible to say which of these divisions can easily be resolved or ameliorated. However, the emotions attached to the ethnic and religious divisions are intense, unrelenting and uncompromising. Many of my Nigerian friends have spoken emotionally about the power of divisive ethnic, religious and political leaders to determine whether or not an innocent young Nigerian graduating from college will ever get a job. Although ethnicity has been a determinant of life success for some time, getting a job in Nigeria today is more dependent upon your religious faith, especially your particular church. People are excluded simply because they don't attend a particular church even though they are highly qualified. These experiences of exclusion have accentuated dislike and suspicion among Nigerians and became apparent to me, when I lived in Europe in the 1990s. A fellow student from Nigerian, with whom I was well acquainted, refused to accept help from another Nigerian simply because he belonged to a different ethnicity and religion. Similar issues are reported in many other African countries. In Rwanda, Burundi, Zaire, Sudan, South Africa, Somalia, and recently in Sierra Leone, Liberia and Ivory Coast, ethnicity has stoked tensions, culminating in national tragedies and failure of governance, and led to the creation of the oppressor within.

The oppressor within

In his work, *Frantz Fanon and the Psychology of Oppression*, Abdullah Bulhan echoes Frantz Fanon in his analysis of Hegel's Master Slave-paradigm and talks about the effects of oppression leading to the oppressor within. The idea is that in the contest between two people for recognition, the winner (the Master) is recognised by the loser (the slave), without having to reciprocate the recognition. In post-independent Africa, the Master (the African political leaders, together with their tribal cohorts) has been recognised by the people (the slaves). However, the Masters have never tried to recognise the slaves, and here it is about citizenship recognition for minority groups and recognition of the survival and wellbeing of the populations. The existing situation, in most African states, reflects the Master Slave-paradigm and perhaps understanding this dialectic might help oppressed people to stand up for their rights. Such an understanding informed the civil rights movement and the fight for political independence in Africa and should be extended to the case of minority groups in Africa.

The remnants of the master slave paradigm remain in the African and half a century ago Fanon made his prophetic predictions about the future of post-independence African states. He observed that the national bourgeoisie is incapable of learning its lesson and could end up denying the people of their hard-won freedom Almost all of the predictions Fanon made about independent African nations have eventuated with spectacular precision in nearly all African countries. Post independent leaders appropriated the colonialist's strategy and employed it as a catalytic tool for destabilising the political relationships between ethnic groups. We have become the formidable tools for self-torture and destruction and the oppression of our own people.

Since independence, the oppression of Africa has entered a new phase, the era of the oppressor within. Franz Fanon's enthusiastic writings about the emancipation of Africa following the independence of several countries in the early 1960s appeared to have been prematurely written because the curse of the oppressor within was yet to unfold across black societies of Africa and the Caribbean.

Fanon's ideas have been described by many people as some of the most important "canons of the black revolution." In early 2011, a Ghanaian writer lamented the lack of practicalisation of Fanon's ideas, and I argued that those noble ideas would continue to remain only ideals to be imbibed at a cognitive level and then pragmatised in different contexts. The fact of the matter is that while Africans have often professed total rejection or ambivalence towards western thought, this has not allowed us to deliver our people from the unforgiving torments of poverty. African independence advocates were examples of leaders who tried to pragmatise the ideas of Fanon by trying to eradicate foreign oppression. However, Fanon's unique ideas about oppression are yet to be practicalised in today's Africa, where the oppressor is within rather than without.

In his lamentations about the oppression of the black man, Fanon philosophized that the only reason why the man of colour is perceived as the "wretched of the earth" is that he was enslaved. To Fanon, it is not the skin colour that is at the heart of the oppression but the very idea that the Blackman was enslaved. With slavery, Africans were dehumanized, subjugated to the position of other people's possession and denied the right to self-determination. Unfortunately, our own forefathers contributed to our dehumanization, and the relics of that spirit to dehumanize our own kind, still fuels our politics; allowing us to carve out systems and structures that oppress minorities in our countries.

Even though many factors are said to contribute to the evils of our African politics, most of them can be funnelled into Franz Fanon's ideas about oppression. Interestingly during Ghana's struggle for independence, Joe Appiah (an eloquent political mind and member of the CPP Party who later became a member of the NLM and United Party) made an interesting remark about Nkrumah's leadership, which highlighted our African leaders' fear of oppression by the colonialists and what is happening today. He said that the Gold Coast was not prepared to substitute a British Raj (Queen of England/Governor of Gold Coast) for a black Raj, in the person of Nkrumah or any other Prime Minister. Joe Appiah's comments/fears manifest in the fact that African oppressors have replaced the colonial oppressors in all 55 African countries. And their role in perpetuating the oppression was brought to prominence by Wole Soyinka's famous question – "what is the colour of the hand that decimated more of its own kind than the white man's?"

African politicians have been oppressing the population(s) since independence, through their control of the discourse on politics, economy and social services, which begets and sustains corruption. Our politicians are able to direct national discourses about who rules and what types of services are provided to communities, depending on ethnic allegiances. They practise and preside over corruption and make unacceptable justifications for their choices in terms of development priorities. Corruption is rife and championed by those in power, who ensure that those who challenge their choices are brutalised. The failure of national leaders to provide basic services to the people goes unchallenged for fear of victimisation and the people continue to suffer the indignity associated with disease, poverty and limited opportunity to develop their potential. Like the slaves in the Master-Slave paradigm, some of the brutalised people seek their revenge on self and everyone else through acts that punish themselves and the rest of society. For the reason that Africans have been brutalised by our leaders, it is so common for people to behave in ways that are completely at odds with common sense. This happens when people endorse corruption and engage in illegal behaviours even with the knowledge that such behaviours will undermine the wellbeing of entire communities. Politicians and public servants stealing government resources meant for public services like hospitals, portable water and electricity is a common practice. It is also common for individuals to steal electricity cables and water-distilling equipment and leave an entire community without drinking water or electricity. Although these acts of internal oppression often have terrible consequences for the entire society, it is profoundly astonishing that those who succeed in such acts are lauded.

These illustrations of the oppressor within abound in many countries and are accentuated by tribalism and corruption. In other words, tribalism and corruption are more at the core of the contemporary African oppression. Tribalism is a vehicle for perpetuating the power of politicians to continue their oppression through the manipulation of the national development discourse and presiding over unconscionable levels of corruption. Tribal and identity politics are used to protect the leaders' treasured machinery of oppression. The ignorance of the African population underpins our tendency to embrace the misguided ethnic/tribal political camouflage of our leaders and to perpetrate oppression against minority tribes. This widespread oppression has certainly led to tribal conflicts, which benefit the oppressors. We need to transcend the oppressive minds directed at "otherness" and support Fanon's dream of elevating the black man from the "floor of the earth". But how is this going to be possible in a situation where extreme focus on ethnicity is necessary to edge oneself into the position of the oppressor?

African leaders as living contradictions

Although ethnic conflicts in Africa are grounded in conscious efforts of dominant groups to perpetuate the oppression of the minority, political leaders have been responsible for sharpening these divisions and the fulfilment of the phenomenon of the "oppressor within". Such a pre-occupation with ethnic promotion, has meant that leaders fail to see what is missing in the national development agenda. Some politicians, in single-minded pursuit of their ethnic agenda have practised ethnic exclusions on a national scale. In some countries land has been taken from minority groups and given to majority groups without proper grassroot consultation. In others, political leaders have intentionally refused to provide social, educational and health services to particular ethnic groups or particular regions as a way of keeping them down.

In playing this role of active exclusion, African leaders not only negated the very idea of freedom and equal rights for which they fought the colonialists but became living contradictions. In essence, not only are they accentuating social injustice of those excluded, they are also obstructing the full development of the human resource potential of their entire nations. Unfortunately, these leaders are myopic and lose sight of the fact that those who are excluded do not contribute positively to the national economy and become a burden to the nation. The excluded groups, who are often poor, contribute to the creation of unhealthy living environments (crime and filth) amidst which the privileged ethnic groups build their gated and high-walled "castles", which dominate African cities. However, no one realises that the "castles" of the privileged, with high walls and barbed wires are actually "prisons" created by their own greed and that malaria-carrying mosquitoes do not need permission or visas to reach them in their privileged "prisons". Thus while they perceive exclusion as only negatively impacting on other ethnic groups, ultimately it affects members of their own ethnic groups.

For Fanon, liberation does not end with freeing the land from the colonizer, but when the psychological freeing of the consciousness of the colonised from the fear of the master, inferiority complex and self-hate is achieved. Unfortunately self-hate is what reigns in the new nations of Africa, with corrupt ethnic oriented politicians as autopressors. The denigration, derogation and oppression (psychologically and materially) of smaller ethnic groups show no signs of abating in many African countries. As the collective values and aspirations of African nations become irredeemably lost, there is less optimism when it comes to realising dream African liberation thinkers of divorcing the black man's psychology from the mental bondage of the past. What is clear is that we cannot fight oppression unless we fight tribalism and corruption.

The inevitable outcome of having national leaders who are living contradictions is that dominant ethnic groups control the national discourses about who qualifies to be a citizen with respect to equality of opportunity and equity in the share of the national cake. African countries are less welcoming of other Africans than our "former European oppressors". Here, we observe the generosity of the European countries in the award citizenship to refugees of any country, while refugees who ever flee to another African country would never be able to dream of citizenship even after three generations. Alassani Ouatarra (President of Ivory Coast) symbolizes such less tolerant attitudes in the recent Ivorian crisis, where his non-citizenship was reinforced, in spite of the fact that all his life's experiences were rooted in that context. In fact the fight for "real" citizenship is at the heart of the conflict between the peoples of southern and northern Ivory Coast and between the Hutus and Tutsis in Rwanda and Burundi.

Chapter 9
Citizenship in Africa

The notion of citizenship encapsulates the idea that one belongs to a place and has the same rights and opportunities as all others. The concept of citizenship focuses on individuals as members of a social community, from which both rights and obligations are derived. In post-independence Africa the notion of citizenship has been contested in many countries. While the specific issues vary from country to country, the biggest problem has to do with marginalisation deriving from ethnocentric castigation of minority ethnic groups.

At independence many African leaders accepted the reality that each of their new nation states, created by an accident of colonialism, had united diverse ethics groups and these arrangements were unlikely to be undone. In essence different ethnic and language groups had to live together. The citizens of the each of the new nations hoped and expected that they would receive their fair share of the national resources and equal opportunity for personal development, in a free country.

Leaders such as Kwame Nkrumah of Ghana, Julius Nyerere of Tanzania, Jomo Kenyatta of Kenya, Kenneth Kaunda of Zambia and Sekou Toure of Guinea envisioned or at least spoke of the need to enshrine equal opportunity and/or egalitarianism in their respective countries. For Kwame Nkrumah the ideal of guaranteeing each man equal opportunity for his development was set in motion in many areas of government, welfare and economic activity. Nkrumah created equal educational opportunity through his massive free universal basic education policy from 1952 and also implementing wide-scale infrastructural development across Ghana. Such resolute pursuance of equal opportunity as demonstrated in Ghana appeared not to have been sincerely pursued in many other African countries. In most instances the leaders lost sight of the fact that they had to govern for all citizens and not just those from their ethnic groups. This created political environments that allowed, dominant or majority tribes to institute and defend mechanisms for the perpetual marginalisation of minority groups, as though they were second class citizens. The result of such structural marginalisation has been violent conflicts and unending civil conflicts. Complaints about citizenship rights and inequality abound in almost every country across Africa

On the basis of such widespread dissatisfaction it could be argued that Equal opportunity, as advocated by early African leaders, has gone largely ignored in much of Africa. And the dream of revolutionaries like Fanon that, the attainment of national liberation must eschew any appeal to ethnicity or 'race' is almost lost. Alana Lentin and Ronit Lentin observe that Fanon recognised the facility with which nationalism comes to be reliant on racism. According to the authors this is evident in Fanon's remark in the case of Algeria that the 'racial and racist level is transcended' (Fanon, 1963: 108) in an Algerian nation that must emerge on the basis of will and consciousness and not on the grounds of shared ethnicity. This act of transcending difference has not happened in most countries and therefore citizenship sometimes has become contestable.

Citizenship is a claim of rights and therefore a legitimate demand by those excluded from access and participation. The idea of citizenship aligns with the concept of justice, which according to John Rawls (1973) is the first virtue of social institutions. From this position, Bernt, d'Anjou, and Houtman, in the work *Citizenship and Social Justice* argue that the violation of conceptions of justice challenges and weakens the moral base of communities. In Africa such violations are commonplace and they are facilitated by the use of the "nationality citizenship model", which according to Kibreab (2003) links nationality and citizenship. The problem with this model is that those without a voice are often excluded from the claim to citizenship. In many countries, majority or dominant tribes do not want to recognise minority groups, even those who are indigenous.

In 2007 African heads of state adopted a resolution in response to the initiative by the United Nations (UN) to adopt a Declaration on the Rights of Indigenous Peoples. The resolution was applauded because it affirmed that 'the vast majority of the peoples of Africa are indigenous to the African continent and should therefore not be denied their citizenship rights. In spite of this declaration many of such indigenous peoples including those who are refugees from neighbouring states are denied citizenship in many countries'. Indeed, since that declaration five years ago, the demands of the resolution are yet to be translated into any practical mechanism for recognising those who are without citizenship recognition in many countries. This inaction speaks to the lack of respect for the rights of those who are marginalised and violates principles of social justice, in particular, recognition and distributive justice because access and participation in many areas of national life are constrained. The perpetration of injustice often happens through the enactment of laws or the manipulation of existing laws by the most powerful groups.

Throughout Africa, citizenship laws have been used in very damaging ways. Bronwyn Manby notes in the introductory chapter of her book "Struggles for Citizenship in Africa" that:

Citizenship law has been used as a tool to get at issues of economic and political power: control of land, commercial opportunities and public office. Extreme violence and discrimination are possible without any abuse of citizenship law to support their deployment, as the 1994 genocide in Rwanda shows. Marginalized groups can be excluded from effective exercise of citizenship rights even if their right to legal citizenship in itself is not contested, notably in the case of individuals subjected to slavery or its contemporary variations, or ethnic groups following a different lifestyle from the national norm, including nomads such as pastoralists or hunter-gatherers.

Bronwyn drives home the negative effects of this marginalisation stating that hundreds of thousands of people living in Africa find themselves non-persons in the only state they have ever known. Their children have no access to recognition at birth via denial of birth registration. This often means that these children who are not recognised at birth are also denied the right to education and access to public health services. In some cases they cannot work because they require work permits and cannot obtain travel documents. And most importantly, they cannot vote, stand for office or work for state institutions. The groups of people who have often been targeted for exclusion are those from ethnic groups that cut across national borders. Also second and third generation migrants from neighbouring African countries also often find themselves out of place.

Population movement has been constant across the continent for hundreds of years and therefore pockets of different ethnic groups lived across ethnic boundaries prior to colonialism and the creation of nation states. Yet the descendants of such ethnic groups have to fight to be recognised as citizens. This problem is quite prevalent in West Africa due to its long history (nearly a 1000 years) of recognised regional trade, inspired by the glorious old empires of Ghana, Mali, Songhai, the Mossi- Dagomba states, Ashanti and the

Sokoto caliphate. These empires covered nearly all of the modern-day nations of West Africa.

The widespread regional trade allowed many ethnic groups to travel and settle in so many different sections of the sub-region. However, when the nation states were created at the close of the 19th century many people began to be defined as "Aliens". Such characterisation was the basis of Ghana's mass deportation order in 1969. Shortly after independence Ghana's economy was booming and nationals of all West African countries were attracted to Ghana. Although pockets of many of these ethnic and language groups had been in Ghana for many generations, they were considered non-citizens. In 1969, Ghana's newly elected civilian Prime Minister K.A. Busia decided to expel people of ethnic groups such as the Yoruba, Igbo, Hausa, Zambrama, who come from Nigeria, Togo, Ivory Coast, Niger and Mali.

Across Africa such mass deportations Africans of different ethnic origins has been carried out in Kenya, Ethiopia and Eritrea and Mauritania. In 1998 following the declaration of an independent Eritrea, thousands of people of Eritrean descent who had only known Ethiopia were deported across the border and their citizenship rights annulled. Eritrea retaliated by expelling people with Ethiopian heritage. There is also evidence President Milton Obote of Uganda expelled Banyarwanda people from Uganda in the 1980s. Similarly the Republic of Congo is refusing to award citizenship to sections of the Banyarwanda people who are considered to be from Rwanda. The government of Kenya has also been harsh on Nubians and some Somali groups who are denied citizenship rights because they are not considered indigenous.

The decade long conflict in Cote d'Ivoire has roots in the historical empires, regional trade and migration discussed earlier. And although some have alluded to the role of the French government in encouraging the movement of agricultural workers from countries such Mali and Burkina Faso to work in the cocoa and coffee plantations in Cote d'Ivoire, the reality is that the new state boundaries did not respect ethnic lines. Many Mossi and Dagara communities inhabit Cote d'Ivoire, Burkina Faso and Ghana and there will be no justification for excluding them from citizenship simply because they constitute a minority in any of these countries. However, this is what happened in Cote d'Ivoire from the late 1990s. The current President of Cote d'Ivoire, Alassani Ouatarra whose father belonged to the Mossi ethic group was excluded from political participation for this very reason. Ouatarra's Mossi ancestors were part of earlier larger Mossi-Dagomba states that once upon a time ruled those areas of Cote d'Ivoire. Yet, the dominant ethnic groups in the south of the country questioned his nationality and manipulated the law to exclude him. He was barred from the presidential election even though he had been the Prime Minister for several years. Many other northern groups who were part of the great empire of the great resistance leader Samory Toure were also denied citizenship and this plunged the country into civil war for a whole decade. The groups targeted for exclusion were not allowed access to national identity cards, and denied all other citizenship rights. The civil war ended with the restoration of citizenship rights to the marginalised groups. However, hundreds of thousands of lives were lost and the economic development of the country stagnated for close to a decade. This also affected neighbouring countries, particularly Burkina Faso, a land-locked country, which depends solely on Cote d'Ivoire to access the sea.

Several reports show that in countries such as Congo, Kenya, Ethiopia and Eritrea, and Zambia laws have been manipulated to exclude prominent individuals and large groups of people living on either side of the defined borders. The most prominent was the case of former Zambian President Kenneth Kaunda. In the 1990s the Government of Movement for Multiparty Democracy (MMD) adopted a new constitution requirement that barred former president Kenneth Kaunda from standing for the presidency in the 1996 elections. The requirement that both parents of any presidential candidate must be Zambians by birth implied that Kaunda, whose parents were originally from Malawi, could not participate in the political process. The intention, as everyone understood, was to disqualify him on the ticket of the United National Independence Party (UNIP), since his parents had been missionaries from what later became Malawi. Such mischievous laws were later used to deport other politicians such as William Steven Banda and John Lyson Chinula.

Another group of people that has been denied citizenship rights are refugees. Thousands of refugees from Ethiopia and South Sudan living in camps in Kenya and Uganda have been denied minimal citizenship rights even though some have been there for decades. In West Africa Mauritania has been deporting large numbers of black Mauritanians and other refugees who have lived there for decades. As Gaim Kibreab in his 2003 work *Citizenship Rights and Repatriation of Refugees* observed, the use of the "nationality

97

citizenship model" which links nationality and citizenship has implied that many refugees are unable to claim citizenship. This departs from the practice in Europe and America where the "new citizenship model" is used. Kibreab observed that resettlement in most developed countries appears to offer better opportunities for belonging than in developing countries of Africa. The basis of entitlement to rights is nationality, not residence…(and) refugees, are denied many civil, economic, political, and social rights accessible to nationals. Consequently, they are marginalised from the life of host societies. In such a situation, as opposed to that of developed industrialised countries, achieving a sense of belonging becomes almost impossible.

Many scholars and researchers focusing on citizenship hold the view that broad and universal citizenship is about social justice. And according to Nancy Fraser in her work *From redistribution to Recognition? Dilemmas of justice in a "Postsocialist" Age*, there is a shift in the notion of justice. I quote extensively from her work in which she eloquently presents the issues and dilemmas around citizenship which fits the situation of contemporary Africa. I use quotes because I realise that I should endeavour not to dilute her eloquent presentation in my attempt to re-interpret it. To Nancy, the "struggle for recognition" is fast becoming the paradigmatic form of political conflict in the late twentieth century. Demands for "recognition of difference" fuel struggles of groups mobilized under the banners of nationality, ethnicity, "race," gender, and sexuality. In these "postsocialist" conflicts, group identity supplants class interest as the chief medium of political mobilization. Cultural domination supplants exploitation as the fundamental injustice. And cultural recognition displaces socioeconomic redistribution as the remedy for injustice and the goal of political struggle" (para 1).

This phenomenon is becoming more pronounced in Africa as marginalised groups who experience near de-nationalisation through systemic exclusion have risen up against the glaring and unconscionable injustice. Nancy then asks a critical question: What should we make of the rise of a new political imaginary centred on notions of "identity," "difference," "cultural domination," and "recognition"? Does this shift represent a lapse into "false consciousness"? Or does it, rather, redress the culture-blindness of a materialist paradigm rightfully discredited by the collapse of Soviet communism? Nancy then advises that instead of simply endorsing or rejecting all of identity politics *simpliciter*, we should see ourselves as presented with a new intellectual and practical task: that of developing a *critical* theory of recognition, one that identifies and defends only those versions of the cultural politics of difference that can be coherently combined with the social politics of equality.

The absence of freedom to claim citizenship in African countries and the marginalisation that goes with it amounts to re-colonisation of the African. And in analysing its effects, Fanon's ideas of freedom become relevant. Frantz Fanon observed that decolonization qua liberation occurs at two levels, (1) the physical level as an act of freeing the land from the colonizer, (2) the psychological level as an act of freeing the consciousness of the colonized from the fear of the master, inferiority complex and self-hate. In essence the struggle of minority tribes for recognition as citizens is justifiable and defensible from the point of view of taking action to be free from the new colonizer- the African dictators and tribal supremacists. This will ensure that there is little room for compromises provided by the "master", which will later on be used as a new foundation for exclusion or marginalisation. Fanon was very critical of compromise and opined that compromises lead to colonized people receiving a "pseudo" or "flag" independent state, where "there's nothing save a minimum of re-adaptation, a few reforms at the top, a flag waving, and down there at the bottom an undivided mass, still living in the middle ages, endlessly marking time" (1968). For those without citizenship rights in Africa, this is exactly how they have experienced African independence for the last 50 years. And their non-recognition implies that our national governments have refused to give back their dignity, as citizens, for over 50 years.

In the face of the reality that ethnic groups in our new nations states will forever now live together, it is high time that African leaders recognised that every minority person has an inalienable right to be recognised as a citizen both in name and in rights. The recognition of rights is critically important because rights not only provide access to resources and opportunities; they also demand duties and responsibilities from the individual to the state. Undoubtedly the realisation of citizenship rights for those currently excluded will crystallize their sense of belonging and inspire honest contribution to national development.

99

PART III: RE-CULTIVATING VALUES IN AFRICA

Chapter 10
Re-Cultivating Values: Return to Indigenous African Values

Introduction:

"If you see that someone is successful in something, the useful question to ask is, how can I do that?"

(A saying from my father Mahama Abu Kuyini)

Marcus Garvey, one of the most prominent black liberation personalities once said that *If an evil mind is determined to evil against another man, no human law could stop it, except a conscience.* This resonates more strongly with each attempt to change the African condition because when a society of people begins to oppress its own, then only conscience can change things around and this is where values come into the picture. The unconscionable level of corruption, "self-imposed torture and suffering that charactarise African societies today can only change when some of those in positions of power, capable of perpetuating the injustices, refuse to use their power to these negative ends. This would require an 'Epiphanic moment', which unfortunately African leaders and peoples are yet to reach. In fact, reaching a collective 'epiphanic moment' could lead us to re-evaluate our values and to develop novel values at the individual, collective and national levels.

Historically, only a few independent African countries, have tried cultivating broad national values to support development. In Ghana, the government of Dr. K.A. Busia started the civics education program in 1969/70, which sought to instil in young people a sense of pride in their traditions and the values of community good /welfare. Unfortunately it was short-lived due to a military takeover in January 1972. Perhaps the most prominent and enduring examples of cultivating universal national values occurred under President Julius Nyerere's Ujamaa Project in Tanzania, which began in the late 1960s. Although Ujamaa had a socialist flavour, the underpinning philosophy was the African notion of community and solidarity. Nyerere succeeded in creating thousands of Ujamaa villages, however, the program failed at a more practical level. Many of Nyerere's critics have laid the blame on his socialist ideals, which did not support food production at a sustainable level. In my view the importance of Ujamaa was its capacity to re-create the values of collective wellbeing in the population and the only problem with the program lay mainly with the process of practicalising its essence. It is here that Nyerere lost sight of the fact that Africans have a strong attachment to their land of birth and so moving people into new settlements was not going to create any sustainable system as a conduit for practicalising the values of Ujamaa. It is possible that if Nyerere had remembered that the African Values embodied in Ubuntu are not about creating new settlements but about creating cognitive change in the society, he would have been more successful.

The Tanzanian experience in any case, shows that cognitive change across an entire country is possible and it is also a valuable strategy for re-valuing Africa. The Tanzanian experience also proves that African nations can generate broad values to propel development. At the national level we need to start asking simple questions such as, "As nations and peoples, what do we want to become? What do we want to transmit to our children through education and of what benefit should their education be to the community? Do we seek nations of people whose skills have no direct positive benefit to our communities, and who indulge in building beautiful houses in a sea of garbage, poverty, disease, dishonesty and greed; pacifying God with their lips in prayer-houses and yet performing no acts kindness? Or do we seek nations of informed and skilled people who have the will and intent to contribute to a common good that touches all people in our local communities?"

In one of his finest and most thought provoking songs *Redemption Song,* Bob Marley asked a very crucial question in reference to the colonial oppressor: "How long shall they kill our prophets while we stand aside and look?" Today, Africa's oppressor is not without but within Africa. The oppressor within is none other than our leaders and ourselves. And perhaps a fitting question we should be asking is: How long shall they kill our children and the future of our children while we stand aside and look?

I have a strong conviction that this generation of Africans can triumph over the ills of the past and emancipate ourselves from the shackles of our corrupt and irresponsible leaders. This can be achieved by developing new values, based on our traditional philosophies of collective wellbeing, such as Ubuntu - a philosophy which essentialises the worth of the individual, those around him, and the value of service. We need to recall that human societal existence, functioning and happiness are determined by the values that hold sway and Africa's existence is and will undoubtedly be determined by our values. I agree with Garry Jacobs and Harlan Cleveland's assertion that the intangible nature of values and the long processes involved in their formation make us overlook their central role in development. For this reason, our African societies are yet to recognise that development is not the overt manifestations of things seen in other countries, but the underlying process of change that involves the creative minds of the individuals of each society. Thus, development as a human creative process can only be realised if Africans recognise that it is ourselves who constitute that potential force for development. This recognition brings with it a responsibility for cultivating an internal inspiration and vision (through the values we hold) to create processes and instruments that allow us to tame our immediate environment for our exclusive comfort first. And I have said in the earlier chapters, no other nation can develop Africa, and the idea that foreign aid (in the forms of food, money etc) is development, is to lose sight of the fact that aid merely an end-product of the creative process, which issue from values the donor nations have cultivated for themselves.

In line with the above, I identify with some development commentators who have argued that establishing proper institutions of government, maintaining the rule of law and increasing educational participation would lead to improvements in the African condition. However, I am also of the firm belief that these actions may not be enough without a strong foundation of enabling values. And we can only create enabling values if we ask the right questions about what has gone wrong in our quest for a better Africa, how other nations have done it and how we can do it. The quote at the beginning of this chapter was a saying of my father, which he often recited to me in the course of growing up. The quote is about asking useful questions and in my view, its essence is one of the key tools, which Africa needs. In analysing the essence of questioning, my father used to say, if you ask "How can I do that" it pushes you to work hard towards discovering what to do and how to achieve that goal. However, if you start by asking "Why don't I have what this person has?", then you are more likely to feel sorry for yourself and less likely to work hard to achieve the same thing. In other words this breeds an emotional rather than a creative reaction. Emotional reactions do not progress our creative process nor nurture our ambition. Thus the more relevant questions to ask are those which focus on how the other person did it and how then you can do it.

These questions are the first steps in the creative process because they stir ambition and a sense of purpose to advance the current situation.

There is a parallel with the African continent here because there is a tendency for many Africans to ask the question "How come he got that and not me?", rather than asking "How did this person or community or nation do that and how can we do that?" In other words, we admire the product and its ownership and the not the process of making the product. This attitude and orientation have to change through a process of values education. Certainly other nations have some things Africa should have or would like to have and the useful question to ask is "How can Africa acquire those things or do those things?" Therefore our leaders and populations, as a collective, need to be asking these questions in order to transform the existing values that appear to generate stagnation. And our ways of thinking must change, in terms of how we see the future of our societies in which our children and children's children will continue to live. At the moment our leaders are not asking those questions but continue to focus their "evil minds" on how to milk our nations, preside over corrupt practices and maintain their oppression of the populations.

As observed in previous chapters the biggest problem with values in Africa is that in the immediate post-independence period, no conscious effort was made at developing broad national values in the new nation states. Prior to independence, the colonial church was interested in developing Christian values in only believers of the faith, while the colonial offices were interested in instilling values that helped them to perpetuate their control and exploitation of the resources. Thus the existing education systems were mechanisms for sustaining the colonial agenda. At the dawn of African independence, freedom fighters and leaders concentrated on the cultivation of the values of freedom in order that the people would rise up against the coloniser. Once freedom and independence were won, it became clear that newly independent African leaders had inherited countries with no common set of values about the kind of societies they wanted to create. The peoples of the new nations held positive values about what makes a good society, but these were fragmented. And as the decades rolled on, very few countries or leaders made attempts at creating collective national values.

The outcome of this failure is that today, there is no African country where politicians seeking government articulate an agenda that includes renewing values that will create a new consciousness around oneness of purpose and collective wellbeing. In recognising that the values of our societies have been gravely eroded, rebuilding these values is achievable through our educational process. This calls for a culture of respect for our societal laws and being conscientious about the effects of our actions on others. It also calls for both our leaders and peoples to completely extract ourselves from the bondage of Affirmative subjugation; to consolidate thinking around traditional philosophies, and the essence and conscience of religious thought/practice.

This Values Renewal Agenda which seeks to cultivate positive collectivist values in successive generations should also eradicate or at least de-emphasise ethnicity in place of citizenship by adopting the philosophy of "Citizen First and Tribe, Second", which will create inclusive nationalism and citizenship. In short, in order to build communities that we all feel proud to belong to, our values should be taken from our traditional African philosophies/values, which enshrine the principle of living for the community. This redefinition will depart from the general idea that development is simply about economic prosperity and in this regard, Africa can draw on the experience of the Kingdom of Bhutan. In the late 1990s the Kingdom of Bhutan proved that it is possible to foster a different notion of development. The country articulated a vision of development rooted in the notion of Gross National Happiness. At The Millennium Meeting for Asia and the Pacific, (October / November, 1998 in Seoul, Republic of Korea) the Bhutanese Chairman of Ministers, Lyonpo Jigmy Thinley made very interesting observations, which relate to the need for values in any society to underpin government development policy. To Bhutan, development was to bring about national happiness in a way that provides a balance between material prosperity and spiritual wellbeing. He said that

"Bhutan's vision of development stresses non-quantifiable goals such as spiritual wellbeing and gross national happiness. We do this through a concerted policy of cultural promotion and the provision of free education, health and other social services. Cultural promotion is one of the four key objectives that we have consistently upheld, over the last four decades. The four major goals are economic self-reliance, environmental preservation, cultural promotion and good governance"

105

These values are inherited from the Bhutanese traditions and it is another clear example of using traditional values to create a positive and promising national vision.

Return to African Philosophies: Ubuntu, Behagu and Burkina

Africa needs to nurture legions of future citizens who will espouse values and principles, ideals and passions, hopes and aspirations that support the building of tolerant and caring societies. African traditional philosophies such as Ubuntu ought to be used as a central governing philosophy, through which values that nurtured our pre-colonial societies as caring for collective wellbeing re-emerges. In other words, Ubuntu and other philosophies, which have been part of Africa's past, could also become the pedestals of Africa's future. The relevance of this is that it enshrines old African values, which are centuries of experience distilled by our forefathers into what Garry Jacobs and Harlan Cleveland call essential and pragmatic principles for accomplishment learned and transmitted to successive generations as a psychological foundation for its further advancement.

The term Ubuntu is an African ethic or philosophy with origins in the Bantu languages of southern Africa. It exists in languages across Southern, central and East Africa, including Botswana, Malawi, Burundi, Rwanda, Kenya, Tanzania, Uganda and Zimbabwe. Variants of Ubuntu exist in all other African languages. In West Africa, the Dagomba-Mossi peoples who inhabit northern parts of Ghana, Burkina Faso and Togo have the terms Behagu and its associated ethic Bilchina or Burkina (from which the name Burkina Faso is derived). The underpinnings of these concepts are similar to the ethic embodied in Ubuntu.

The broad essence of Ubuntu is the strong relationship between the worth of the individual and those around him, and the value of service. Archbishop Desmond Tutu, in his Book, *No Future without forgiveness* defines the person who has the quality of Ubuntu as one who is open and available to others, affirming of others, does not feel threatened that others are able and good, is based on a proper self-assurance that comes from knowing that he or she belongs in a greater whole and is therefore diminished when others are humiliated or diminished, when others are tortured or oppressed. He goes on to explain that Ubuntu allows a person to say with

106

confidence that "I am a human because I belong. I participate. I share.... In essence, I am because you are".

The prominent Malawian philosopher and theologist, Reverend Sindima and other writers described Ubuntu as also embodying the notions of the child as the child of the society. This notion of the child as belonging to society is linked to the traditional African concept of community, a mix of the divine, scared and the mundane. The community transcends the people who live in it at any one moment. The individual belongs to the community in life and death. The individual's rights are tied to the obligations he fulfils to the community. This is the exact opposite of today's nation states where individuals instead expect the community or government to fulfil specific obligations to the individual without a comparable reciprocal obligation from the individual. The old notion of responsibility to community was fundamental to the idea that people in the community were only poor if the entire community was poor. In other words, one could not be in absolute strife because he could always ask his neighbours for help. Ubuntu underpins this thinking.

Former South African President Nelson Mandela after explaining the philosophy in relation to corruption in leadership said that Ubuntu does not mean that people should not enrich themselves, but "Are you going to do so in order to enable the community around you to be able to improve?" The essence of this question as I see it is that Ubuntu should lead to the improvement in the lives of other people around African national leaders, the ordinary people in our societies.

In West Africa, the concepts of Behagu and Bilchini or Burkina, which come from the Dagomba-Mossi languages are philosophies related to Ubuntu. Behagu represents the notion that a person has values, which respects the dignity of others. It also denotes a sense that a person has a sense of responsibility, strives for community good and solidarises with other people as a way of making himself and his family an example for others. On the basis of these principles, strangers are to be taken care of and included in the family and community as much as possible.

A related ethic is Bilchini or Burkini/Burkina, which is associated with the values of Honesty, Integrity and Hard Work among the Dagomba-Mossi groups of West Africa. A person who has this quality demonstrates honesty and integrity in all their actions in addition to hard work for family and community. In 1983 when

107

Thomas Sankara became President of the then Upper Volta, following a coup d'état, he sought to invigorate broad traditional values in the population. He therefore identified the traditional Mossi-Dagomba philosophy of Bilchini or Burkini /Burkina and renamed the Country Burkina Faso, which means the land of the people with Honesty and Integrity or "the land of upright people". Sankara was keen to ensure that ordinary people would live by the philosophy of honesty, integrity and hard work as way of improving the general wellbeing of the population. Although his vision was driven by traditional philosophy, it had an overarching communists flavour and this perhaps led to his undoing and assassination in 1987. Sankara had a vision, but his assassination in another coup d'état meant that he did not live long enough to nurture that vision. However, this important philosophy like Ubuntu is at the disposal of Africans and can be used for the full benefit of coming generations.

Since independence, the values of honesty and integrity have not necessarily been taught as values essential in themselves in the many African countries. However, they are extremely important values because they constitute an indispensable foundation, upon which several other values are built. For example Bilchinsi or Burkini as a value system is related to the Protestant Ethic and the Islamic value of working rather asking begging for alms. The protestant ethic has been the bedrock of the work ethics of Christians in Europe, America and Australia, but only a few Africans have it as part of the ingrained values of their Christian faith. It is therefore important to unearth our own traditional philosophies, which are similar to this ethic to remind the next generations of the pragmatic approaches to our collective wellbeing. If African societies make Burkina and Ubuntu into an overarching value, they will be conveying a strong message to the Churches and Mosques, to which we are trooping, that honesty, integrity and hard work are values that God requires of people who worship Him.

Reverend Harvey Sindima in his 1995 book '*Africa's Agenda: The legacy of liberalism and colonialism in the crisis of African values*' expresses the view that instituting the philosophy of Ubuntu across Africa has the potential to provide a new set of values for new generations. Indeed in my view Ubuntu could lead to rediscovery of our traditional notions of community, which can be broadened beyond our villages and ethnic groups to our entire nations. The very idea that we could see our nations like our local communities also implies that we could re-evaluate our perceptions of individual responsibility to our nation states. Finally it could lead to a new definition of citizenship, and aspirations for equality of opportunity for each and every one and a match towards improved wellbeing.

The Botswana Example

Recently Botswana has envisioned a nation that will cultivate a strong sense of the traditional African values based on the philosophy of Ubuntu or Botho in Tswana. To the Tswana speaking people Botho means a person is a person through other people and this has been made part of the Botswana Vision 2016 Agenda. As a country that strives to create a unified and egalitarian society where the wellbeing of everyone matters, the country's government has brought the philosophy of Botho or Ubuntu to national consciousness by including it as one of the key pillars upon which its future will be built. The inclusion of Ubuntu or Botho to her development principles such as Democracy, Development, Self-Reliance and Unity, demonstrates a unique commitment to creating a more inclusive society. In her Vision 2016 agenda, Botho is defined as a process whereby people wanting to earn respect must first give it to others. Botho reminds each person to gain empowerment by empowering others. It encourages people to applaud rather than resent those who succeed. It disapproves of anti-social, dishonest, disgraceful, inhuman and criminal behaviour, and encourages social justice for all. This quality is expressed as "Onale Botho" in Tswana

During a recent visit to Botswana I noticed something remarkably different from my native Ghana and other West Africa countries. Customer service in public offices was smooth, with little or limited delays or dilly-dallying. The Batswana provide service within the Ubuntu or Botho principle of *I am a person through you (the other person) who is seeking my service.* This guiding principle accounts for the fact that in Botswana the money extracting culture of the Civil service personnel, which is pervasive in many West African countries, where Civil Servants expect you to give them money before they provide you with a service, was completely absent. My research colleague from the University of Botswana explained that the Batswana don't do such things and in my opinion Botswana has been able to institute and maintain Ubuntu or Botho based values at a national level. I reckon we are witnessing the evolution of a country unique from the rest of Africa, where looking after one another is more ingrained in a proud and caring people. The positive outcome of this philosophy around collective wellbeing accounts for the fact that the country's huge national resources have been managed in a way that allows citizens to have near equal access to services. Africa should therefore look at Botswana as model when it comes to pursuing a national values agenda.

Ubuntu and citizenship in Africa

Ubuntu as a broad and encompassing philosophy will also support the development of inclusive national citizenship as well as remind us of the conscience of religion. In previous pages I explored the issues of intolerance of our ethnic differences, marginalisation and a near de-nationalisation of minority groups and observed that these have become a matter of glaring and unconscionable injustice. I also highlighted Nancy Fraser's advice that we should see ourselves as being presented with a new intellectual and practical task of developing sound and pragmatic agendas of recognition and socio-political equality. Ubuntu as a philosophy can help us achieve this by adopting the principle of Citizen First and Tribe Second. This principle, which I refer to as reversal principle implies that individuals see themselves first, as citizens and then second, as tribes. Such a principle will support inclusive nationalism and citizenship at a practical and interactional level, so that the universal citizenship legally bestowed by national constitutions will become grounded psychologically and socially. It will also foster strong commitment to the progress and wellbeing of entire nations and local communities. It is important to remember that the experience of marginalisation is a recipe for the development of egocentric and individualistic feelings that give birth to greed and corruption.

The absence of freedom to claim citizenship in African countries and the marginalisation that goes with it amounts to re-colonisation of the African and African leaders must recognise that every person who has right to citizenship ought to be recognised as a citizen both in name and rights. This includes the right to access resources and opportunities but in return also demands that citizens honour their responsibilities to the state. We need to develop the value that it is not acceptable that some citizens have to negotiate and advocate for an opportunity to receive their inalienable citizenship rights.

Finally, Ubuntu will allow African states to embrace, in their conceptualisations of citizenship, the notion of distributive, retributive and recognitive justice. Recognitive justice is very important in Africa because it will serve as a strong foundation for an expanded understanding of positive regard for social difference, the centrality of the socially democratic processes and distributive justice. These conditions will become the solid foundations of inclusive nationalism and citizenship in which redistribution and recognitive justice lead to the unquestionable acceptance of minority groups, as people with unique needs, In this way, African governments will be ensuring similar outcomes for all citizens, an act which will lead to what Nancy Fraser (1997) calls transformative remedies to inequality.

Ubuntu, Conscience of Religion and Collective Wellbeing

A very important component of re-valuing Africa is undeniably the spirit of religious practice. As observed earlier in this book, religious practice that concentrates on prayer without a concurrent emphasis on the essence and conscience of the religious thought will only culminate in misery for self and society. In fact the need to look at the conscience of religious thought is paramount once we understand that almost all of our actions are self-directed from the engine room of cognition, where we make judgments about the consequences of each action. Morality as we see it has a pathway to the inner part of the individual–the conscience. However, since we cannot successfully legislate morality, we should instead endeavour to cultivate it in order to keep moral values alive, to guide our actions. Thus, keeping our conscience alive, as part of religious practice in Africa is fundamental to our ability to sustain the argument that religion is of some relevance in Africa. George Washington is credited to have said "Labour to keep alive in your breast that little spark of celestial fire called conscience."

The conscience of religious thought will let us see that what we do to our fellow men, as leaders or ordinary citizens, has a more profound effect on their lives than the prayer we say for them. Through decisive action we have the power to create and implement laws which adhere to the principles of social justice and ensure equality of citizenship, equal opportunity and other forms of distributive justice in African societies. The welfare provisions in Europe and America that allow even the poorest people to have some level of support in their lives derive, in part, from the conscience of Christian religious thinking. In Africa where historically such provisions have also been made, the greed of powerful leaders and their cronies has ensured that the principle of universalism enshrined in those provisions has never been realised. To a large extent such actions are borne out of the fact that the perpetrators of exclusion either do not possess, or refuse to take on board, the conscience of their religious teachings at the cognitive and pragmatic levels. Ubuntu as a core philosophy will remind us that our nations and communities are a mix of the divine and the mundane and that collective wellbeing matters.

Chapter 11:
Affirmative Values

From Asia's Affirmative Orientalism to Africa's Affirmative Africanism

Affirmative Orientalism, a term coined by Robert Fox (1992) emanates from the critique of the work of Edward Said titled "Orientalism". Some scholars have criticised Said and made the case that he failed to see the positiveness of the oriental discourse. Robert Fox (1992) argued that Said's theory fails to account for the Orientalist discourse's enabling of anti-colonial nationalist resistance against western domination. In this regard, Fox discussed the nature and scope of the Indian liberation movement against British imperialism in the early twentieth century and wrote that western Orientalist discourse's pejorative stereotypes of India evolved into "Affirmative Orientalism" (p. 152). According to Fox, Affirmative Orientalism was an oppositional discourse that transformed the negative image of India into a powerful source of cultural and political empowerment. Takayama and Apple, writing on the oriental discourse in 2008, explained that in Affirmative Orientalism, anything that appeared in Eurocentric Orientalism as India's ugliness and weakness became India's beauty and strength, which Indian cultural nationalists then employed for the cause of anti-imperial movements.

The notion of Affirmative Orientalism provides a foundation for re-defining western culture as abnormality and Asians have been able to use Affirmative Orientalism in a positive way and managed to entrench the beauty and uniqueness of oriental thought and culture in the psyche of western thinkers. Affirmative Orientalism is about developing values and identities that solidify a positive view of the self, taking actions not only to support this self-image, but to pragmatically realise the objectives of this mindset. In Asia, Affirmative Orientalism underpins the drive to excel in all facets of life and in domains of knowledge such a science and technology, something that has been championed /dominated by the west in the last 500 years. The Japanese have imbibed and mastered American and European ideas and then transformed these ideas into an oriental ideology as the foundation for their astronomical industrial success. Now China and India have followed in these footsteps. Equally,

Malaysia and Indonesia are rapidly advancing in science and Technology.

Keita Takayama writing about the Japanese version of Affirmative Orientalism noted that the philosophy has consistently appeared in the discourse of Japanese cultural nationalism, or so-called Nihonjinron (discussions of Japanese uniqueness). This discourse characterises Japanese society as group-oriented, harmonious, ethnically homogeneous and reliant on shame. The values of *Group Harmony* and *Avoiding Shame* are two powerful forces that drive the manifest social solidarity and the creative endeavours and exemplary achievements, which are characteristic of Japanese society today.

The relevant question for Africa is: *Is there an Affirmative Africanism?* As far as I can see, the answer is "No". Rather, what we have is what I have called Affirmative subjugation, which must be eradicated. An African version of Affirmative Orientalism, which should be called Affirmative Africanism, should re-funnel thoughts and actions into the traditional African value of living for the good of the community inherent in the philosophy of Ubuntu and Behagu or Burkina.

It is important that Africa adopts Affirmative Orientalism or Affirmative Africanism not as a dialectical process but a pragmatic process backed by action. If the philosophy is adopted at face-value or in the realm of dialectics, then it will suffer the same fate as the notion of Negritude propagated by Aimé Fernand David Césaire (1913 – 2008), Leopold Sedar Senghor (1906-2001) and Leon Damas (1912-1978) in the early part of the 20th Century. Césaire was Frantz Fanon's teacher in his home country of Martinique and influenced Fanon's ideas. Bulhan (1985) notes that Fanon (as a Blackman) had adopted Aime Césaire's notion of Negritude to calm his own psycho-existential crisis. He declared that his black ancestors had built great civilisations and therefore the white coloniser was wrong and resentful about the past achievements of people of colour. However, Jean Pierre Satre's words in the preface to Leopold Senghor's book *Anthology* left Fanon deflated. Satre is said to have argued that Negritude was the root of its own destruction because its adherents failed to realise that it was simply a transition, not a conclusion, a means and not an ultimate end. In other words, pride in Africa's past will be relevant if we can use it as foundation for further development.

In the same fashion, Affirmative Africanism should be seen as means to an end; a value position that fertilizes the seeds of related

114

value systems that can be transformed into actions for Africa's progress. The Asians have not stopped at the dialectics of Affirmative Orientalism. In particular China, Japan and now India, have not simply boasted about the greatness of their civilizations in the past, they have also pursued scientific and technological development relentlessly over several decades in a manner that has now seen them at par with Western industrialised nations. And they have not stopped there, but are pushing forward in all other domains with the aim of establishing some dominance in the world economy. The network of value systems that is at the heart of the Asian success is what Africa requires, and needs to instigate at a more specific and pragmatic level. It requires Africa to understand how Asian societies (with collectivists cultures like Africans) think and what specific values they conjure to the fore when they educate their younger generations. How they have managed to maintain their traditional religious beliefs, in spite of some sections of their populations becoming Christian and Muslims; how they have managed to prioritise mastering their environment (to improve wellbeing) rather than prioritising the notion that they are now the true warriors of some foreign religion such as Christianity and Islam, ready to kill and die for these faiths.

In general African cultures are traditionally collectivist rather than individualistic, similar to most cultures across Asia. However, if one considers that collectivist cultures like China and Japan and Korea are making very prominent strides in economic and technological development against the stagnating situation in Africa, one is certain to wonder what is wrong with Africa. As indicated before, the roots of the stagnation cannot be laid completely at the foot of colonialism. It is also about values, which are internal organising principles that direct human energies and determine the course of individual and social development. And as pragmatic principles for accomplishment transmitted by society to successive generations as a psychological foundation for its further advancement the values held in today's Asia and Africa appear to be different.

Richard Nisbett discussed the nature of human thought in the introductory chapter of his book "The Geography of Thought", which alludes to how values differ due to how we think. He narrates that one of his brilliant Chinese students once said to him "You know, the difference between you and me is that I think the world is a circle and you think it's a line" [....]. The Chinese believe in constant change but with things always moving back to some prior state. They pay attention to a wide range of events; they search for

115

relationships between things; and they think you cannot understand the part without understanding the whole. Westerners live in a simpler more deterministic world; they focus on the salient objects and people instead of the large picture; and they think they can control events because they know the rules that govern the behaviour of objects" (p. xiii). Nisbett notes that, he was sceptical about the idea that people from different parts of the world could be different in the way they think. However, upon further reading of the comparative literature on the nature of thought written by psychologists, philosophers, historians and anthropologists (from East and West) he realised that apart from psychology, other disciplines believe that Westerners and Easterners (Asians) have maintained different systems of thought for thousands of years. Westerners assume that the behaviours of objects –physical, animal and human – can be understood in terms of straightforward rules. They have strong interest in categorisation, which helps them to know which rules to apply to the objects in question and that formal logic plays a role in problem solving. Asians on the other hand attend to objects in their broad context and understanding events always requires consideration of a host of factors that operate in relation to one another in no simple deterministic way (p. xiv).

Nisbett concluded that these assertions were revolutionary and that the social scientists were implying that people from different cultures differ in their "metaphysics" or fundamental beliefs about the nature of the world; the characteristic thought processes of different groups differ greatly; and that the thought processes are part of the beliefs about the nature of the world. People use the cognitive tools that seem to make sense –given the sense they make of the world. "..If people really differed profoundly in their systems of thought – their world views and cognitive processes – then differences in people's attitudes and beliefs and even their values and preferences might not be a matter of different inputs and teachings, but rather an inevitable consequence of using different tools to understand the world"(p. xiv).

It has become apparent that although this may not be wholly true, thinking patterns in different parts of the world are due to environment and culture. My observation of today's Asian students has led me to the conclusion that the focus of their thinking is slightly different from African students. My personal experience and habits about knowledge seeking which I believe is common among African students is the tendency to think globally. On the other hand Asian students add a dimension of specialisation, with a strong motivation for mastery (*I stand to be corrected*). They focus or concentrate on a single area or specialisation and try to become a master of, or expert in, that endeavour. What is the importance of this analysis of thinking patterns? It is to help me propose a return to the value of mastery in Africa.

Value of Mastery

The motivation to become a master of an endeavour (an art, skill or a field of study) or being the best at what you do has psychological and socio-cultural roots. Psychologists believe that individual motivation for self-esteem is linked to the need to achieve competence and a sense of mastery. To Abraham Maslow in his hierarchy of needs, achieving mastery is part of our social and affiliation needs. Thus this purely individual desire to be a master of some endeavour is linked to the social environment and that is where social values about mastery come into the picture. In other words if a society values mastery of some skill, then children growing up in that environment will learn that it is important to master that skill. In this sense, if one compares African societies of the past to the present, we can see that something has changed.

While the motivation for mastery was common to both African and Asian cultures prior to colonialism, such motivations for mastery have vanished in Africa. Whereas in the past young Africans endeavoured to be masters in some traditional activity or functional area, today interests are geared towards employment and making a name for yourself as someone who is rich or has high position in society. It is so common to hear people talking about the importance of personalities and not about how particular skills and societal functions can be improved.

Pre-colonial African societies specialised in specific arts and skills. In some ethnic groups clans were based on these specialisations. For example the Yoruba, and Hausa of Nigeria and Dogon people of Mali specialised in different trades. And the same applies to the Mamprusi- Dagomba-Mossi groups, where specialisation was based on clan trades and arts. In the past, children born into Dagomba clans such as Blacksmiths, Drummers, Barbers or Butchers, had to work hard to learn the trade, the hierarchies of the clan, the clan dance and the meaning of the clan music. It was a disgrace not to know all these things and for this reason, young children had to aim to be the best in the entire clan. However, the coming of western education changed all that. In fact the value of mastery in African societies changed with Western Education because the aim of the first educational institutions was to teach simple literacy and numeracy skills that led to employment as lower paid non-specialist labourers. This generated enthusiasm for generalised western education skills to secure a job quickly and little concentration in specialisation and mastery. Educational progression with the aim of developing creative thinking in African graduates was not instituted until after independence in the 1960s when many higher education institutions were established with creativity and discovery built into the agenda of educational pursuits. By this time the African mind had been programmed to think of western education as purely about white-collar jobs only.

The desire for mastery evokes strong drives for creativity around a particular subject matter or skill area and leads to advances in that domain of knowledge. Western scientific and technological advancement has always hinged on the drive for mastery and it is still promoted through education. However, Western education in Africa eradicated this mentality or value in many places. As the traditional methods of production and life became less useful or adored, people's aspirations and desire for mastery changed. Thus the loss of one of the central tenants of living in local community affected the aspirations of African people. In Asia, on the other hand, the philosophy and value of mastery did not completely die and so many Asians are still keen to be the best in what they do. They take great pride in picking up an idea and becoming the best in it. This is not to say that Africans don't do this, but it is less widespread today. And this, in my view, accounts for the fact that many Africans have a more broad knowledge of things and less specialisation and therefore are not often outstanding persons in different fields. The effects of these developments and conditions have resulted in a pattern of thinking among contemporary African students. In my opinion, most African students want to think of several, varied and diverse areas rather than one. They therefore develop a broad understanding of the different things and not necessarily a mastery of one single endeavour. In other words, knowledge seeking is often about what I need to learn to avoid the inconvenience of not knowing, or to avoid the unpleasant and dangerous situations or to get by or to earn a living. In short, African students' motivation for learning is far removed from the need to champion the extension of the boundaries of knowledge in a field.

Deriving from the above analysis is the apparent need for re-valuing Africa through nurturing and sustaining values in young Africans to aspire for mastery or become the best in particular endeavours or domains of knowledge to improve our communities. This will also propel individuals and nations to generate ideas and products to benefit the world. Such a direction will also enhance African nations' capacities to build happier communities and support improved collective wellbeing. These types of values that are required for change are currently not effectively taught in schools. Values such as honesty and service for the good of community are nowhere demonstrated for the young to emulate. If civil servants must receive money to do their work for which they are paid and contractors are unanimous in their belief that shoddy jobs are good provided those are government jobs, then our children will never learn any values of benefit to our society.

We aspire, as nations, to be like Europe first, and second to be ourselves (Africans). If we employed what I elsewhere called the reversal principle, then we would need to be first Africans who have mastered our environments and sincerely value the progress of our communities. In this way, we would first and foremost endeavour to explore and develop pragmatic ways of dealing with or taming our harsh environments, and utilise every drop of our creative powers to harness our unique resources to stop hunger, disease and uplift our living conditions. For the simple reason that some solutions must have a unique African focus, this is the way forward, rather than trying to be like Europe and America in one giant leap.

We need vocational education with a local community orientation. I argue that we are choosing the wrong philosophical premise for our educational reforms by seeking to channel our school graduates towards entry into the global market, rather than enhancing the quality of life in the local community. Our young people are shunning the existing technical / vocational education programs, which appear to have no meaningful bearing on improving our infrastructure and ways of living. Therefore, very few of our young people have the skills in industry that could be used to directly improve the quality of local community living and the infrastructure we are building for our future. Our survival and comfort have to do with mastering our immediate environments in a way that allows us to make maximum use of all types of resources including foods, herbs and other unique local materials. As Africans, our environment is unique and useful to us first, and to all others, second. Thus no other persons/societies should or can do the mastering of our environment and resources for us, and no one in the western world is

119

ever going to seriously help to develop our local foods, plants and herbs for our exclusive utilisation on diseases that are unique to us.

In the face of these, our vocational education should have a pronounced local community orientation. Such an orientation would ensure that the types of plants, foods, infrastructure, skills and services required in a local community form the basis of the vocational education curriculum. Take the examples of the depressing reports associated with the African families and individuals in Zimbabwe and South Africa getting access to land for the first time in decades. Many of the land owners have not been able to turn those lands into productive resources to improve individual wellbeing and contribute to economic growth. Unfortunately no one in Government is seriously (and I underscore "seriously) thinking about creating a comprehensive policy around training, technical and business to ensure that these lands are utilized as sources of economic growth and by extension improved wellbeing. How many more years are the governments of South Africa and Zimbabwe going wait before some meaningful action is taken? Poor and irrelevant education is in itself oppressive and given that most African people under colonialism had poor education there is an essential need for deeper thinking from our governments about using education to improve agricultural production but it has to include a new set of values.

More recent world maps of water resources show that Africa has huge underground reserves and yet we are thirsty. These water resources can be utilised for economic progress and our education systems should become the vehicles propelling this growth. For example comprehensive education/ skill training around composting, irrigation systems and dam construction should be part of vocational training programs in all localities where such services and skills are part of the community's economic life. Teacher training should then focus on the capacity of teachers to adapt their teaching methods in ways that bring out the creative powers of both students and community institutions to improve on the methods of harnessing local resources.

This type of focus already takes place in the areas of agriculture in some African countries, but it is often piecemeal and has no links with other sectors such as health. A regeneration of local community oriented values and agenda is needed now to redirect vocational education to train graduates that can develop and manage our land and water resources and synthesise knowledge of our local herbs into a collective portal of viable treatment options for diseases in our communities. We need to creatively use our resources and dispel the illusion that we cannot use our resources for anything meaningful. The reality is that we do not escape from poverty and disease by having skills, which are comparable with others on the world stage, but mean nothing for our communities. We do not also escape from these ills by building nice homes in filthy, diseased environments. We forget that we can never be truly happy and free until our environments and communities become free; for the mosquitoes and bacteria do not need visas to travel from the dirty mud-huts of the poor majority into the modern European-style homes of the rich and powerful few. We would benefit, in terms of overall progress (good health, security and happiness), if our houses were mud-huts in communities that value our common-good through the provision of sanitation, food, education, drinking water, and basic health care. In this achievement we will see the true spirit of the philosophy of Ubuntu.

References

Alana Letin (2008) De-authenticating Fanon: Self-organised anti-racism and the politics of experience. In Alana Lentin and Ronit Lentin (eds.), Race and State, Newcastle: Cambridge Scholars'Press, 2006, 2008). Retrieved from http://www.academia.edu/279096/De-Authenticating_Fanon_Self-Organised_Anti-Racism_and_the_Politics_of_Experience

Ali A. Mazrui (2005) The Re-invention of Africa: Edward Said, V. Y. Mudimbe, and Beyond *Research in African Literatures* 36, (3) 68-82. Retrieved from http://destee.com/index.php?threads/the-re-invention-of-africa.45025/

Bernt, T., d'Anjou, L. & Houtman, D. (1992) Citizenship and Social Justice. *Social Justice Research*, 5, (2), 195-212

Bradley, Lloyd. 2000. Bass Culture – When Reggae Was King. Penguin. ISBN: 0-140-23763-1

Chris. Potash, (1997) Reggae, Rasta, Revolution – Jamaican Music From Ska To Dub. Schirmer Books. ISBN: 1-901526-09-7

David Katz (2003) Sold Foundation – An Oral History Of Reggae. Bloomsbury. ISBN: 0-7475-6847-2

Denise. A. Isom (2007) "Performance, Resistance, Caring: Racialized gender identity in African American boys", *The Urban Review*, 39 (4), 405-423 Retrieved 21 November 2012 from http://link.springer.com/article/10.1007%2Fs11256-007-0061-y?LI=true

Edward Vasicek. (2011) How a Worship Format is Destroying the Evangelical Church. Retrieved from *http://www.sharperiron.org/*

Frantz Fanon (1961) The wretched of the earth, Grove Weidenfeld, New York

Gaim Kibreab (2003) *Citizenship Rights and Repatriation of Refugees*, International Migration Review, 37 (1), 24–73 DOI:10.1111/j.1747-7379.2003.tb00129.x

Garry Jacobs and Harlan Cleveland (1999) Social Development Theory Retrieved from http://www.icpd.org/development_theory/SocialDevTheory.htm

Godfrey W. Robert. (Online), Worship: Evangelical or Reformed? Retrieved from http://www.opc.org/new_horizons/NH02/04e.html

Hussein Abdullah Bulhan (1985 *Frantz Fanon and the Psychology of Oppression*, New York, Plenum Press

Jarle Simensen (2009) Africa: the causes of under-development and the challenges of globalisation. Retrieved from http://www.regjeringen.no/en/dep/ud/kampanjer/refleks/innspill/afrika/simensen.html?id=533474

Joyce West Stevens (1997) African American Female Adolescent Identity Development: A Three dimensional Perspective. Child Welfare, 76(1): 145-172.

Keita Takayama and Michael Apple (2008) The cultural politics of borrowing: Japan, Britain, and the narrative of educational crisis. *British Journal of Sociology of Education*, 29(3), 289–301.

Kwaku Asante-Darko, (2000) Reggae and Pan-Africanism http://www.arts.uwa.edu.au/MotsPluriels/MP16OOkad.html

Leela Gandhi (1998). *Postcolonial theory: A critical introduction*. Edinburgh: Edinburgh University Press.

Michael De Koningh and Mars Griffiths (2003) *Tighten up! – The History Of Reggae In The UK*. Sanctuary.

Michael E. Veal (2007) *Dub – Soundscapes & Shattered Songs In Jamaican Reggae*. Wesleyan University Press.

Monte Wilson (2010) Narcissism Goes to Church: Encountering Evangelical Worship. http://www.yuricareport.com/MindAndSoul/NarcissismGoesToChurch.html

Nancy Fraser. (Justice Interruptus. 1997) From Redistribution to Recognition? Dilemmas of Justice in a "Postsocialist" Age, Routledge 1997; Retrieved from http://ethicalpolitics.org/blackwood/fraser.htm

Nzau Wa Musau (2010) African thought: Did the Greek's plagiarize our philosophy? Retrieved from http://musau.blogspot.com.au/2010/03/african-thought-did-greeks-plagiarize.html

Peter O'Neill, Frank Muhly, Jr. and Peter Schmidt (1988) The Tree of Iron **http://www.der.org/films/tree-of-iron.html**)

Roderick J. McIntosh (1999) Africa's Storied Past, Archaeological Institute of America, Volume 52 (3) http://archive.archaeology.org/9905/abstracts/africa.html

Stuart Hall, S. (1981). Notes on deconstructing 'the popular'. In R. Samuel (Ed.), *People's history and socialist theory* (pp. 227–240). London: Routledge & Kegan Paul.

Stuart Hall, S. (1990). Cultural identity and diaspora. In J. Rutherford (Ed.), *Identity, community, culture, difference* (pp. 222–237). London: Lawrence and Wishart.

Richard E. Nisbett (2003) The Geography of Thought: How Asians and Westerners Think Differently – and Why. London, Nicholas Brealy Publishing.

Richard Fox (1992). East of Said. In M. Sprinker (Ed.), *Edward Said: A critical reader* (pp. 144–156). Oxford: Blackwell.

Ronald Toshiyuki Takaki, (Ed.) (1994) From Different Shores: Perspectives on Race and Ethnicity in America. New York: Oxford.

The Willie Lynch Letter (online) http://www.finalcall.com/artman/publish/Perspectives_1/Willie_Lynch_letter_The_Making_of_a_Slave.shtml Tunde Adeleke in his work (2009). *The Case Against Afrocentrism* Jackson: University Press of Mississippi.

Ulysses Ronquillo (2010) Reggae, Hip Hop and Black Nationalism. http://da-what.com/2010/03/11/reggae-hip-hop-and-black-nationalism/

Valentin Y. Mudimbe (1988) The Invention Of Africa: Gnosis, Philosophy, and the Order of Knowledge, Indiana University Press Yaacov Shavit, (2001) *History in Blac: African-Americans in Search of an Ancient Past*, Frank Cass Publishers

ABOUT THE AUTHOR

Bawa Kuyini was born in Bimbila, Ghana and is currently engaged as senior lecturer in Social Work and Education at the University of New England, Australia. Bawa attended school in Bimbila, Yendi and Tamale in Ghana before completing a Bachelor of Education (Hons) Degree at the University of Cape Coast, Ghana. He taught at a Teachers' Training College and a secondary school for some years. In the late 1990s, he studied Social Work at Volda University College, Norway and worked as social worker for the Asker Local Government, Norway until 2001. He then completed a PhD in Education at the University of Melbourne, Australia. As a teacher and researcher on educational and social issues, his research interests are in special /inclusive education and social work, including child rights, disability, refugees and migration.

Music and sports, especially Soccer and Hockey are key leisure activities.

www.ingramcontent.com/pod-product-compliance
Lightning Source LLC
Chambersburg PA
CBHW081106290526
45795CB00006B/2020